Dear
Earl

Thank you
for your Support

Sandra

From

Federal Prison

To

First Lady

Tamika Riley - McReynolds

Shadegreen Publishing and its affiliates recognize the importance of preserving what has been written, to print the books we publish on acid-free paper and we will continue to produce excellence.

THE LIBRARY OF CONGRESS HAS CATALOGED THIS MANUSCRIPT EDITION AS FOLLOWS:

Riley -McReynolds,Tamika 2018

From Federal Prison to First Lady

Copy right © Tamika Riley - McReynolds 2018

All rights reserved.

(Paperback)

From Federal Prison To First Lady

"Lessons Learned"

ISBN 978-0-9911257-2-2

LCCN 2015957340

Cover design by Lushbrand

Published by Shadegreenpublishing

Editing & Layout by AJHouston

Printed in the United States of America

From

Federal Prison

To

First Lady

Tamika Riley - McReynolds

This Book is Dedicated to My Husband

Pastor John H. McReynolds

CONTENT

INTRODUCTION

Writing this book for the last 10 years has been a personal project in the making. I wrote it as a tool to help me better understand myself. I felt this project will one day assist a young person going through a storm. The process taught me how I want people to treat me, how to treat others and how to keep it moving. This experience was a lesson for me and I accept everything that came with it whole-heartedly. I pray when someone reads this book they will gather something positive from it. During the writing of this book there were times I felt like giving up and putting the pen down, but my God would not allow it. I battled heavily with recounting one of the darkest periods of my life. Somehow through the darkness I started to see little specks of light emanating from the pages and I was able to see my purpose for writing these words a little clearer after a while.

Writing my story, made me feel like I was a medical doctor because of the many emotions that rose to the surface. I honestly didn't know I still held on to so much of the pain deep in my subconscious. Some of the issues remained because I had not forgiven others. I discovered there were still lots of anger, sadness, disappointment, and I was just plain mad at the world for this injustice. I try to never hold my feelings in, anyone who knows me knows I express what I feel and speak my truth always. Always have and always will. One thing I can honestly say is, I love Tamika Riley! I currently have no regrets, and I am still learning to forgive.

Going through a Federal Trial and going to Prison was terrifying and confusing because I did not know why this was happening to me. I could not grasp or comprehend the details behind each charge. One day my god brother now deceased, said to me "why not you?" I almost cursed him out but then he explained, he said "Tamika, God chose you, for no one else could have done it your way." I thank God for carrying me the whole way in his loving arms. This experience will stay with me forever. It reminds me of the woman God chose to go

11

through this adversity, he never left me for one minute, although it felt like at times I was baring this burden alone.

I want to continue to grow from past experiences that helped to shape me into the woman I am today and be successful while doing it! I had to let some things go, including family and friends that were not worthy to walk into the next chapter of my life. I had to learn to delete people from my list of companions and be ok with my decision. Some people are truly out to hurt your character, your integrity, and are not happy seeing others close to them succeed. You must know you are a priority, and that you matter! Always believe you can be any-thing you choose to be. You must learn to keep negative people from trying to block your blessings because what is for you, is for you! I want this book to encourage young people to do their very best in whatever they choose to do. We only get one life, so please make the best of it!

Redemption Is For Everyone

-Tamika Riley-

FOREWORD

We met at St. Aloysius High. I think I was a Junior and Tamika a freshman. I introduced myself with this grand introduction. She returned the same energetic hello that I had given her! Everyone else's hello was either soft spoken or low tenor but Tamika's greeting was soprano like mine. She had the kindest spirit. We became sisters that very day! I'm the loud, funny, dramatic sister and she's the over the top, funny, and don't even try it sister. This balance has served our friendship for over 30 years. Our parents refer to the other as daughter. We laugh, we argue, we disagree, and we love just as sisters do.

Tamika's book titled "From Federal Prison To First Lady" will help so many women and young adults move from an unforgiving space when life changes in an instant. Her mental strength will help open your eyes to look through a lens of gratefulness, positivity and hard work. Tamika has always lived her life out loud and has an overzealous and giving heart.

Tamika, in your stillness you became an author, writing a book that teaches as well as gives truth to a heartfelt thought provoking experience. You documented your journey while actually going through the process of unimaginable hurt, healing and forgiveness. The healing power of your words in "From Federal Prison To First Lady" screams redemption and finding Godly love within. You never gave up and you never let anyone around you give up. Your gift of motivating others to reach their destiny shifts the reader from victim to survivor.

After reading "From Federal Prison To First Lady" others can get a glimpse of who Tamika Riley McReynolds has always been; the Boss Chick from Jersey City who is still rocking it out for her community, family and friends. Once you start reading her private thoughts, you envision how you too can turn any life altering situation into a positive outcome with confidence, faith and work. Not just physical work but reading how she works on forgiving herself while still providing an honest viewpoint while angry was brave, moving and courageous.

Her story is just as important today as it was ten years ago. Read this page turner taken from handwritten journals as she documents challenges and lessons learned through unconditional love and perseverance. I am so proud of Tamika and honored to serve in bringing this story to life. It has been an amazing journey for you and it's only the beginning. Tamika pushed everyone involved with this project to give their absolute best.

If you are tired of the same outcome, then live your dreams out loud just like Tamika and write it down. Keep motivating all of us! Tamika is like our Oprah! I love you sis.

Francine Dawkins (ShadeGreen Publishing)

aka Cham

"To whom much is given much is required"

From Federal Prison To First Lady

Chapter I

Tamika's Story Her Way

"Lessons Learned"

It was a muggy hot summer day in Jersey City, New Jersey the perfect weather for a Sunday morning. The choir is following the Pastor's lead with the song, "I Need You" by Bishop Hezekiah Walker. The Pastor is in the pulpit ministering to the large congregation, telling them today he came to a conclusion concerning his personal life in marriage, while repeating the words by Bishop Hezekiah Walker... "I Need You." The church folk started whispering and looking around to see if the Pastor had lost his mind, because they have no idea where he is going with this message about a wife! Then it happened, Pastor John H. McReynolds asked the question while the congregation listens attentively- "Will the next Mrs. McReynolds, PLEASE STAND!" That question sends tidal waves down the aisles of wooden bark as if paper was being made. Time stopped.

This is when I Tamika Riley stood, dresses as sharp as always. Fashion beaming from head to toe. That particular Sunday, I wore a black skirt suit. The Jacket stopped mid waist, accompanied by an elegantly stitched pencil skirt with a slight slit at the back of my knees. The outfit was accented by six-inch black stilettos, with a black and white striped church hat tilted slightly to the left. And my black silky hair covered most of my right brow. This is my signature, my name, my journey as I stood and proceeded toward the altar of redemption. In that moment, I saw God's glory through stained glass. He said; "I will give you double one day for all you went through, and the story is your service to the children, many others forgot about." For those who comment and judge others but do nothing for the children in the inner city, shame on you! Within a few months after arriving home from federal prison, I arranged for the children of Mt. Olive Baptist Church to tour the White House. This is what I do. This is who I am. I am Tamika Riley McReynolds. This is my story of love, redemption, and lessons learned.

Born and raised in Jersey City, New Jersey was far from glamorous, especially in my neighborhood. My parents are Linda Riley and Arthur Brookins. On March 25, 1969 Tamika Sermone Riley came out of the womb as an Individualist. I attended PS #20 grammar school and graduated from St. Aloysius High School. As a teenager I was involved

18

in as many activities as I could possibly handle. I graduated with honors, member of the National Honor Society and was always willing to help others by tutoring students who needed extra help. I started traveling during my freshman and sophomore years with the help and guidance of my parents. My mom would say, there is a whole world out there baby, and you have to go get yours. My mother and father were never together but together they raised me to be the woman I am today. I was very blessed to have my dad around; a lot of my friends didn't have a father figure or dad around growing up. My parents always instilled character in me, molding me to be the best person I could be, despite where I lived. They didn't play games when it came to my education. Oh yes, spankings, whooping's, whatever you want to call them were given out freely if you brought home bad grades. I made sure I worked hard on my grades and stayed on my P's and Q's when it came to school. Unlike my brother who chose to be the class clown and kept getting in and out of trouble. One thing I know is, my parents wanted the best for my brother and I.

At 16 years of age my family suffered a tragic loss with the death of my cousin, who was killed by someone evil who thought he had the right to take a life. My mom had to make a quick life changing decision in taking custody of her two children now left without a mother. If my mother did not take them in, they would have gone to foster care. I have always admired my mother for opening her doors to raising two young children. This taught me strength of family and the power of a strong woman. My mother, Linda taught me to go for my dreams. I tried to pitch in where I could and help take care of two babies even at 16 years of age. This lesson taught me not to take life for granted because anything can happen and to be prepared mentally to stand on your faith in the mist of energy draining trauma. Time does heal some wounds and the decision to step up and take custody of two young children was admirable. Not many people would have done that. It was not easy, but we made it work even when other family members were against the decision. I realized later that watching my mother stand up for what she believed in during such a sad moment taught me how to stand when facing adverse situations. I watched family members turn on my mother, I saw how people can really be and it was a huge lesson to learn as a teenager. I've always had this outgoing vibrant spirit and greeted others with warmth and love because I am genuinely happy to make another's acquaintance. I like people, but this lesson taught me not to trust those closest to you. It only takes one thing bad to happen for one to see who is down for them, who is not and who is truly a friend or a hater.

Helping to raise my two little cousins made me realize, I did not want children of my own." This experience made me aware of how hard it is to raise children in this cruel world. It is hands down one of the hardest jobs in the world. I pray we played an important role in their lives as adults now that they both have families of their own. They were young then, and don't remember the sacrifices that were made on their behalf. And don't remember during their time of great loss, other family members wanted to give up on them. During this time of grief and hardship it made me want to stand up for the underdog when any child or group of children could not stand or speak for themselves. This is the motto I stand firm on till this day. I want young people to win! There is so much good in them. The world teaches them to hate. I want them to make it regardless of gender or race. We must be the ones to teach them how not to make wrong decisions because there will always be consequences. Lesson learned, lessons taught.

Moving forward into my young adult life. I attended college and begin traveling to exotic places. One thing I can attest to is, I had no fear of trying new things and experiencing new places. I worked for Sterns, UPS, and then Continental Airlines all before I turned 25 and while attending school. I was fortunate in my early 20's to move to Maryland and start a career as a manager with UPS. I applied for my first apartment and the first car I purchased had to be delivered because I didn't know how to drive a stick shift. I learned quickly because I had to get to work in my new drop top whip! These are just some of the life experiences that helped to build my character and make me into the person I am today. One thing I must say, I am not afraid of anyone except Jesus! While developing my professional portfolio in my twenties, I also had a personal life and became involved with a very jealous and controlling guy. He was jealous about the smallest of things, and carefully watched every move I made. I knew this was not the type of relationship I should be in and wanted out. I realized I had to leave even if I loved him. Tamika had to leave the building!

I knew I wasn't your average chick just by the creative things I was doing. At the age of 16, I arranged for UTFO a hip-hop legend to perform "Roxanne Roxanne" at St. Aloysius High School. By age 18 I was designing my own jean collection called Martini Classic Jeans. I opened a boutique in my late 20's called the Fashion Dome in Newark, NJ. I applied for a permit to shut the street down in downtown Newark, NJ to have a runway fashion show in the middle of the street. After servicing a few high-profile clientele, media publications became my passion. I was a high profile publicist during this time. So, I have over 25 years of experience in this game.

I have always had outlandish dreams and was driven to be productive, I needed to be able to make a statement without saying a word. My life felt fulfilled because I took risk as a young entrepreneur. I believe you must believe in yourself, no matter what others think of you and to do it with strong will and tenacity. In doing so you can show young girls they can make a difference at any age. Now, it is up to you to make things happen, what are you waiting for? Lesson learned, lesson taught.

Journal Entry: *November 1, 2010*

I don't have to write every detail about the trial and who did what. What I do want the reader to capture are the lessons learned. The past is the past and hopefully I can inspire just one young person to learn and grow from some of my mistakes. We are all human and of course we will make mistakes, but the healing comes from your for-giveness and service afterwards. Find your redemption. I wrote this book while in the mist of the trial, while serving in federal prison and completed it when I returned home. Each time someone ask me or in-quired to others saying, "where's her book" my famous line became "Go catch a case and write your own book". One of my best friends who I call my sister laughs so hard every time I repeat this mantra, be-cause others may want to say when it's your time to move on some-thing, listen, only you and God know when it's time. Stop telling every-one your business and do you. A lesson learned.

A knock at my door happened around 2001 when the FBI came to my home inquiring about a 911 investigation. I invited them in and they stayed about 10 minutes. They stated they were covering the area. That was the last time I saw or spoke to the FBI until another knock at the door in 2007 at an ex-boyfriends home. Let's just say this was the beginning of my hell, my story, and my journey. The incident helped me to transcend in understanding that one significant life changing lesson could blossom into so many lessons I will never forget. I must say, that particular situation was something that required a much higher strength to depend on. It is very important having real friends and family in your corner as I did, and I am truly grateful. I want to be very clear if it's something I did, because I believe in taking full responsibility for your actions. I never wanted to be a blank canvas for others to paint a picture of wrongdoing and I loud mouth Tamika not be able to defend myself. My rebirth came with every page turned to complete this book, giving you raw nuggets on life lessons in how to avoid bad vibrations when they are around you. Answering the ques-tion, what to do when you're trying to find the meaning of an experi-ence to learn from it? I needed to finish my story my way.

You can relive the trial if you want to read the transcripts, but this book is about second chances, God's Mercy, favor on my life, and lessons learned. Young people need our blue print in being transparent about real life, not reality TV. Some deliverables I wanted to share in this book did not make the edit. It consisted of a lot of cursing, and name calling. I was angry for a long time. I thank my husband for praying for me consistently and helping me to know God's forgiveness. I can tell you, he is the real deal, I am truly thankful for his covering. I will touch on this in greater detail in a later chapter.

The items and characteristics listed below are just some of the items I wrote down prior to picking up a pen. I reviewed this list every time I made an entry in my five-subject notebook. This book includes important dates as entries were made on those specific dates explaining how I mentally got through the process whole and intact. The lesson learned will follow. This is the focus of this book so if you had other thoughts of what it would be, remember my quote "Go catch your own case and write your own book"-Tamika Riley McReynolds.

This trouble began with the HONORABLE and being accused of getting property from the City Of Newark, let's be clear if I would have lied on the Mayor this case would have went another way...

CHECK THE TRANSCRIPTS. Let me say this, you cannot get no property no where unless it goes thru the City Council....Here it is a ghetto chic from Jersey City just trying to make a difference and lands up with a Federal Case. WHAT THE HELL IS THAT!!! I always remind people before they start running their mouth, check the facts. We are quick to throw stones and try to hurt one another. I refused not to hurt the HONORABLE Mayor Sharpe James, because again HE did not do anything to me. The one important fact I learned real quick I knew what Tamika Riley was made of. I am so blessed to have went through this darkness because GOD removed all the trash from my life. During this period I brought a lot of garbage bags....

I really thank God for the squad that surrounded me and let me know that I was a factor. The darkness was here but God always provided some light for me to see....

From my trial over ten years ago, the lessons learned can assist in helping adults whose spouse may be incarcerated and help the child involved trying to find ways to deal with the separation. It not only affects the person in the situation, it can affect the whole family. My husband who was my fiancée at the time, and a few friends I will acknowledge later, were also hurt by the outcome as I was doing ten months in Alderson Federal Prison. The end of my story is really the beginning, because after marrying my husband, John H. McReynolds and becoming First Lady of Mt. Olive, I learned how to walk in forgiveness. He is also my Pastor, so I am covered on all sides. My husband knows there is a calling on my life. Everyone who is close to me knows this too. When you are granted a purpose for being here and you don't operate in that gift, it can lay doormat inside you screaming to get out. I never heard that scream because I always stayed working on my dreams. Lesson learned; the words you speak over your dreams have meaning. Speak life into yourself.

My personal relationship with this man opened my eyes regarding the following;

Stand for what you believe in

Loyalty

Integrity

Friendship

Forgiveness

Loyalty: Many have no idea what this word means. I am true to it and always have been. I was ready to expose friends that lied on me and tell their secrets but over time, the revisions in forgiveness started to happen each time I would write. I even had family turn their backs on me once I had to stand trial. I learned quickly some of the closest people to me wanted me to go to prison. "Once you know better, you do better". You can forgive a person and never speak to them again. It's just that simple. Sometimes you have to learn to let others go and love them from a distance. A lesson learned.

Integrity: I earned strength I didn't know I had when I had to withstand every day of the trial of the century. I had to fight for me because no one else will fight for you like you. My attorney, Gerald Krovatin and the dream team were a Godsend, to help me with this fight of a life time. I stood up for what I believed. My life is important to me; when you are in a fight for your life, you can't come with your tail tucked between your legs. You will have to fight for your rights! I was facing ten years. What are you facing right now that you need to get up and fight? Make those phone calls, do the research, and watch God open a window in heaven and pour out blessings you won't have room enough to receive. A lesson learned.

Friendship: True friendships stood the test of time and they are still a part of my team. Sometimes it is hard to forgive those that have done you wrong. You must allow God to work on your heart as you forgive yourself for trusting those not worthy to go the distance in your life. Watch how your trust is renewed as new ventures open and new lasting friendships emerge. A lesson learned.

Forgiveness: Forgiveness as stated above is a process. It is hard watching those close to you lie directly in your face, that was an eye opener for sure. All I could think of was how I put those same people in position when it came to creating their own business or building a team to help the children of Jersey City. Stand, no matter what. Faith is the substance of things hoped for and the evidence of things not seen.

Going to Prison was a life changing wake up call. Either I was going to fight, or I was going to die. I have always stood for what is right and what they were doing to me was wrong. I made the choice to fight, not lay down and rollover and let these people tell me what I did wrong. No way, only God can do that. I may be crazy, but I ain't anybody's fool! Throughout the trial and in the end, I had to trust and believe that joy really does come in the morning. I was taught a valuable lesson.

Chapter II

The FBI & The Knock

Journal Entry: November 15, 2010

 Well, well, let me start by saying thank you to everyone for their sincere prayers and not telling my story for me. This book is to give you something from me that no one was able to give. My story, my way, as so many people spoke negatively while having no idea what they were talking about. Why do people do that? Talk about things like it's the truth just because it was in the newspaper. I want my readers to learn from the lessons I was taught, and the trials God allowed me to go through. No fake story, no lies, just my truth. Let's begin my story.

 This knock at the door came after I returned from Las Vegas. I was in town for a huge event, taking meetings and networking. There were three federal agents standing at the door, as I peeked over their shoulders I could see a handful of agents waiting outside. Now, me not knowing I should not have spoken with them without an Attorney present, (what did I know?) I thought it was fine because I personally didn't have anything to hide. Well Ok, back to the knock! I was at my ex's house and the FBI knocked at 5am on his door looking and asking for me. Me not knowing any better, I opened the door to find out what they needed with me. They questioned me for about four hours without representation and then wanted to search my office, TRI Public Relations Firm located in Newark, NJ that I created with plenty of help in 1999. Still I had nothing to hide and didn't think I would need an attorney. The FBI searched my office which was framed with pictures of entertainers I had worked with, such as Neyo, Jarule, Russell Simmons, and others. They packed up fourteen boxes and carted them away. I was devastated to say the least. The whole time I could not understand what the hell was happening. Why did I have FBI agents at my PR Firm that my team and I had worked so hard to establish? All the questions were geared toward the former Honorable Mayor Sharpe James. They asked the same questions over and over. I still didn't understand; still not clear what was really happening.

Well, me being naive and needing clarity, I went to speak to the FBI on my own. No representation from an Attorney, like a big dummy! Of course, I know better now but first and foremost; anytime the FBI comes to see you and ask you any questions you should immediately get an attorney. Even when you have nothing to hide. You see it on TV every day, someone without representation is setting themselves up. Take my lesson and learn from it. Get an Attorney always!

For the record, having a personal and private relationship with the former Mayor was definitely not right on my part. I have owned up to my error in judgment because I knew he was a married man. My error, my judgment, my repentance... still it was not against the law, not the right thing to do I know, but not illegal. The government and whoever else tried to make something that was not. It left me feeling broken. My life was about to take a drastic turn, I would have to fight for my life because they tried to give me over 10 years!!!!

The knock at the door by the FBI came as a surprise. Who the hell would have thought the FBI would be knocking on my door. This whole ordeal felt like a bad dream and I was never going to wake up. Around 2001 or 2003 the FBI came to my home and spoke to me briefly regarding terrorist. I did not think anything of it until I received the knock in 2007 by the three officers. This nightmare was getting worst by the day.

Journal Entry: *November 16, 2010*

The book from the beginning had to be written not only for myself but for others. You must sit back and count all lessons and learn from them. Be able to teach one when you make mistakes, be able to give back what you learned so others can avoid making the same mistake.

The beginning of my life turning upside down started with those knocks at the door. You never know who is going to knock at your door, especially when it's the FBI. Now before I start this book, this is my story, my way. It's not about bashing or destroying anybody's character. It's my story regarding the lessons that I have learned and have been able to teach to others. In the beginning, before I started to really understand why in the world the FBI should be knocking at my door. This experience I went through was for me and only for me. When things happen like an earthquake or your life shatters right before your eyes, you must know one thing and that is you will get through it. When this journey started I never thought a personal relationship with someone I considered a friend of mine would turn to no words during the trial. Never in a million years would I have thought I would be on channel 2, 4, 7, 11 or even Telemundo... go figure. My dad always said; "this is the hand you have been dealt, now play it." Now that being said, this is a powerful story that changed my life in so many different dimensions that sometimes I cannot keep up.

Just for the record, I never wrote a book in my life, so I hope you understand this had been a long journey just to be able to write the events, the pain, the anger, the betrayal, into words. One thing I want to express through this experience, is when you know the truth it does not matter what anyone else thinks. Life is so much better when you ask God to guide you and make your path clear. The opinion of man goes out the window. A lesson learned.

This book is a defining moment in my life that changed forever. What do I mean? For starters, I am a single, Black, African American Female that was doing the damn thing! I was living my dream of starting my own business, doing wonderful things in the community for children, a PR Firm with celebrities, traveling, and dating. In a blink of an eye, it all fell apart. Then came the media, then the trial, then prison, then marriage-Hold up! What just happened!!! It's called Life, just keep on living and you will understand exactly what that statement means! A lesson Learned.

If you are reading this, you have probably heard about the Tamika

Riley trial. By the way, I still do not know how in the world it became my trial, but it did, so I had to deal with it.

This all began with the choices I made. I was taught grown people do grown people things. The decision of dealing or associating myself with a married man was my choice only. I want to be very clear, there was no intent to hurt anyone in the process. During the short period this man was in my life, there was mutual respect and an endearing work relationship. He taught me things I will never forget as a woman. I knew he cared about me and he was not out to cause me any harm, as I was to him. He was a confidant, he was a friend, he was someone I looked up to during the friendship that turned into a brief affair. It was a learning experience that I will never forget. For the record, no matter what people say, or what the media reported, I was there, I know.

First lesson I learned, people will talk about a situation even if they were not even in the same state. This is when I learned some people just talk to hear themselves talking. A Lesson learned.

I am not going to make this into a negative situation. I want this to be what it is my truth concerning this big life changing event. For a second lesson, I did get discouraged in the beginning. Having thoughts of would I make it back to live my best life or when will it be complete. The lesson, the true lesson I learned from messing with a married man; I should not have; bad move yes and once again I give my apologies to his wife. Our mistakes are for us to grow from, the lesson is to teach others to do better. It is our job to help change the mind set of young people through small doses of truth. We are not here to waste our being, we have a purpose.

By the way, it took me a long time to get here, because I have drafts of this book in so many different versions. It started to help channel my anger but going to jail helped me to deal with it. It helped me to truly value Tamika Riley on another level with myself, and not lose my identity while in prison.

When I made the decision to deal with this man, I never

thought in a million years I would go to jail for it. Never thought, well, it's not a thought it's a fact, I went to jail and no I did not like it. Yes, you are going to have some residual anger because I was not healed at the time I was writing this book. God is handling that department. Going through this period of my life starting from 2006-2007 changed me inside. I felt sick every second of the trial, every minute, every day, but I knew deep down in my gut, God was going to get me through but how he was doing it, I did not know.

The knock reminds me of having an outer body experience. I could not believe they were there to talk about another individual. When this happened, I just felt the whole time I was dreaming! Guess what? It wasn't a dream and I better get it together quick, before it turned into a nightmare.

Let me set the stage. This nightmare started based on me and my personal dealings with a man I know cared about the community. It was business, I not only handled properties, but community events and trying my best to make a difference in the lives of youth. Not one word was mentioned about that during the trial or put in the newspaper beforehand. We fed families every Thanksgiving, brought celebrities to the community events in downtown Newark, provided fashion, photography, and a Teen Magazine Program opportunities throughout the State of New Jersey.

For the record, all procedures were handled by city government offices; this gentleman had nothing to do with my projects or with the properties (check the receipts). Please keep in mind I was there. This book is not to make you believe in the events that took place but to give you my story my way. This gentleman and I again had a brief relationship. You find people that make a difference in your life where the impact is unforgettable. The media, the behind my back talking tried to make this trial, the trial of the century. Unless you sat with me in that court room you have no idea what I had to deal with, so go sit down over there somewhere.

Young people speak what you know, not what you think. Do not get caught up in the hype of anything.

The trial was not about me and that was made clear early on, because I could not understand how the media could report what was not true. I was in PR, so I knew how media worked but I learned just because the media reports it doesn't mean it's true. It's the truth, this is when I had to put my boxing gloves on to keep myself protected mentally.

I sat in Newark Federal Court which felt like forever. I do not wish this experience on my worst enemy. If you don't stand for something you will fall for anything, that statement is the truth. Well, of course I didn't get it right away but after a couple of months went by, you better believe I got it! A lesson learned. God made me smile every time I thought about him. At one point I thought I would never smile again. Going to court every day after getting arrested in July 2007, the game began. Tamika Riley, the ghetto chic from Jersey City, is all over every channel, all over the world, over a million hits on the internet and in newspapers. Then I thought at least I had something to do with the economy. I helped some people stay employed. This was a good thing, right?

It's one thing to report the truth about me, at least let it be true. I was in disbelief when I was arraigned, I had 13 counts against me. I did not understand, but I thank God for my "Dream Team", Gerry Krovatin and his team. They saved my life! They were truly a gift from God. I called him Gerry, a God send!

I could not understand 13 counts from having a brief relationship. I could not grasp it. Still to this day, I don't get it, but now I understand. When I tell you, I thought I was in a movie. I went to court every day during the trial. I saw people lie, I saw people put their hand on the Bible and still lie! I saw people that I did not know, lie. Go figure! I didn't understand sometimes, but that trial kicked my ass. I did not know if I was going to make it with the lies being told, the betrayal of friends and people wishing you go to jail. I didn't understand this lesson.

This trial changed me. It opened my eyes to PEOPLE! People are there when everything is going well but when I caught my case you would have thought I never met these people that was supposed to be my friends and family. People loss their memory, they got lost, and they act like they don't know you.

Journal Entry: January 28, 2011

Bishop Hezekiah Walker song, "God Favored Me" got me through some rough times. You know when you hear your song at a club, at the block party, or in the car? Well, this was my song during my journey. I didn't know Bishop Hezekiah Walker at the time, but he doesn't know 2007 until the present, this song plays in my brain. It was the words that kept me going on my painful journey. This experience hurt, it made me cry, it kept pain on my heart, I was aching, I was angry, and I didn't think I could forgive those who tried to hurt me!

Chapter III

Pain & Healing

You know I learned a valuable lesson during my media circus about my friends. I thought I had friends for life! Instead I found I had friends that wanted your man, friends that cheated on their husbands, friends that were always there for the limo rides, shopping sprees, concerts, events or just having a good time. When I caught my case, I discovered they were the ones who were truly jealous of the life I was living. They were wishing and hoping in some deep way they could be me. It's sad, I know for a fact they were wishing I went to jail. It taught me a life lesson in loyalty. I always gave it but didn't receive it from the people I thought would always be loyal friends. It doesn't matter if you had been friends for 1, 5, 10 or 20 years, people will reveal their true nature during your hardest trials. All those years, I thought they were in my corner, in the end they turned out to be haters! They are the true definition of a hater. Not only did they benefit, but their children reaped the benefit also. Somewhere in the midst of the struggle they forgot. Their memories got lost, but they did not forget to show up for every event; who does that? The answer is, my fake friends - no character, no loyalty, and absolutely no integrity. If you don't believe it, catch a case and see who stays in your corner. The lesson for me was the trial removed what wasn't for me. I did not have friends. I had people that wanted what I had instead of being happy for me, but now I know. Thank God for those remaining. Do not ever give up on your beliefs and your morals. I learned everyone can not be in your circle, they can't have a front row seat or even share the same stage. When you know your value, it does not matter who or what tries to get in your way. Keep it moving, stay focused, and don't change who you are for nobody.

During the trial I met someone. I did not want to get close to anyone else especially during my media exposure. Well, it was not up to me. I know for sure it was a God thing, not a Tamika thing. This trial opened my eyes to how God did not give up on me. He sent me someone, because he knew I was going to need a lot of prayer. Who would have thought I would go from Mayor to Pastor? Not in a million years. It was not up to me. That's when I started to realize. God already had the playbook on the table. I met this man when I was going through a situation with another man. So, it's like I could not finish one relationship or one event that needed closure before God intervened. Even though the relationship had been over with the Mayor, I was left facing 13 counts because of it.

When the Pastor and I met, I never expected to be his wife. I never thought I would be anyone's wife for that matter. I would like to dedicate this to my Husband, Pastor, John H. McReynolds for being the one person that did not know me from a can of paint and stood by me. Even after telling him I would probably be going to trial and possibly going to jail. After we made it through that difficult time, he treated me like he knew me for years! He walked all the way with me better than the people I had known all my life. He picked up where I deleted fake friends. We were friends first. He gave me so much insight, wisdom and understanding. I never thought I would be able to let him in my personal space, at least not with all the drama I was going through. He was willing to ride it out with me no matter what the media said. I know he has my back. The number of phone calls he received would make you think he was in the courtroom every minute, but he never came, he was just there in spirit. He is a true man of God. Pastor did not judge me. He weighed the evidence and sat down with my attorney to ask questions. I would frequently ask; why are you willing to take this journey with me? My baby will always say, because I know. I would have said "what do you know"? He knew I was the truth too, that's what he knew.

Lesson: I did not know how much Pastor was truly connected with God. Let me be clear. I do not know all the scriptures in the Bible like anyone else. I am not a holier than thou type of person, but I do know God for myself. Being with the Reverend helped me with my faith and my walk made me a stronger woman in Christ. A lesson I'm continuing to learn.

I asked these questions of my husband in 2007.

How did you know?

When did you know?

Why did you fight for me?

and Why did you believe in me?

   We were married soon after my return from prison, at Mt. Olive Baptist Church. I will go to bat for that man. He held me down when there were not many willing to stand with me, and we are still holding it down together. Lesson learned, trust those that are willing to fight for you 100 percent. That is called unconditional love.

Journal Entry: *February 7, 2011*

The biggest fear I experienced during this period of my life, was going to trial and then going to prison. All the while I had visions of arriving back home and completing this book. It was scary to me because I never had the opportunity to write a book and tell my side of the story, giving my perspective of all the lessons learned. This is a big thing to be able to write, think, and to walk in these healing moments of forgiveness. I had no idea writing the different chapters from a portion of my journey would feel completely different than talking about what happened. Writing my truth of the situation has been very therapeutic. Sitting in my own space and revisiting everything encountered during the most trying time in my life, has been critical in helping me to come to grips with it all. Although some of the memories are still painful. I know you should not fear anything or anyone but God! Sometimes feelings can rise up inside of you, but you must learn for yourself how to deal with them, always remember, God or whomever your higher power is, will have your back. A very special person once told me, if you don't hurry and finish the book, it will land on a shelf in the dollar store and no one will read it. We laughed so hard and I quickly got back to writing the uncompleted chapters. It has been hard trying to put it all together explaining all of the lessons learned and trying to grasp everything that should be included in the book.

Journal Entry: May 11, 2011

This book has been the only conversation worth having, re-garding my pain, heartache and my lessons learned. I started over so many times. I never thought the book would ever be completed. Being open minded, being in the moment, I felt I needed to start over for the next 31 days to really be clear about what I wanted to write. This is all new to me, but this is an opportunity that I truly know God gave me. I found by being so laid back about completing or continuing to finish the book, I had to say to myself; make it happen and do not let any-thing get in your way. I am so happy that my experience will have the ability to change someone's life. It has taken longer than I planned but after reading, thinking and being quiet on matters regarding my book, it hit me that I had to put the finishing touches on these final chapters of my life. This book is my way of doing just that.

I learned never to degrade myself when someone else spoke poorly of me, it was my job to speak life back into myself. I want the readers to get something positive, no matter how nasty my trial was. I owned up to the situation, I walked away with a true sense of self, my integrity and my loyalty. I lost friends and gained a new best friend. If nothing else, during the trial, what I consider to be the worst time of my life also effectively changed my life. It was like a bad toothache that no dentist could pull or get rid of. It felt like forever.

The introduction of Tamika Riley begins with, I have made some mistakes and I also have learned from them. Some of the mis-takes inspired me to become an author and revealed some facts that you did not receive. For the record, one thing I truly believe is when trouble comes no matter what, you fight for what you believe in. Even if you have to stand alone. If you are right, do not let anyone try to block you. Speaking mainly to our young people, stay focused! In life you will make mistakes concerning who is in your corner. Listen to your gut instincts before they disappear on you while you are going through hardships. Start noticing that silent hate but don't live there. Live your life but watch your back. No matter what the situation is, fight for what you believe in.

Whatever you heard from the press, media, tv, and radio leave that on pause and get in your reading position. One thing I know is when you and only you know the truth nothing else matters. The beginning of my dream Ms. Riley, the one and only, this story is for me to tell.

How the hell do you get indicted and your closest friends disappear! Still to this day I do not know how this word became a part of my life, Indictment. So how did I arrive in a Federal Court room in Newark, New Jersey? Never mind local, I was in Federal Court, indicted, went to trial, found guilty and sent to prison. Absorb all of that, before I go any further. Please digest and try to understand everything written in that statement. To top it off most of your friends and family turn against you.

In the beginning all the decisions I made I firmly stand on them. I do not regret anything I have done but I have learned so much through those who smile in your face but are hating behind your back. You may have someone like that on your job or in your family. There is nothing but drama every time they are around. Pay attention for those are warning signals from the earth to have the necessary conversation and / or step away from the friendship. This trial was mine, the mistakes were mine, going to prison was mine. I had to learn these lessons in order to move into my purpose.

The journey of my life taught me the real meaning of loyalty, friendship and forgiveness. There are few people today that will have these characteristics. Although some of them will present themselves as real friends but when things happen, like the FBI comes knocking at your door, they automatically get amnesia. When limos are picking them up, or when we are going on trips, or shopping sprees, everything is lovely. Please let me be very clear. I never once said to my so-called friends; "be there for me, go to jail for me or even talk to the Judge for me." I always believed they would be there for moral support. People *will portray to be one thing and when pressure comes they will reveal their true nature. I cannot take fake people pretending like they are on tour. Please go sit down somewhere.*

Journal entry: June 14, 2011

Let's get some of the chitty chatty out of the way from the haters.

Here are the facts:

I had a brief affair with the Honorable

I got indicted on 13 counts

I went to trial for 20 something days

I went to Prison in West Virginia

I kept media employed

I fought hard for my life

I am still standing

I am still doing what I love to do in helping other people. So now that we got the facts out the way. Let's begin. This book is to share what I learned from the trial. This book has helped me emotionally to understand myself full circle. I had so many moments that I felt it was time to share in my own way. This opportunity to write a book is huge, it's big for me! I think the reason it did not come out sooner was because of me not being mentally ready. Well, we are here, and I am ready. Please let's be clear. Let me say it again, I have never written a book before, so this is my first. Let's get through it together, I hope and pray that someone will learn something from my experience. My main goal or only purpose is to share my story my way, not the way the Media portrayed me and for people who don't stay in their own lane. I really hope adults get something out of this also, but my passion is helping teens succeed. Hopefully they will grasp a little something from a sister that looks like them, talks like them and grew up exactly like them. Also, this book has become a healer, a source of real information and a guide for me to continue to stand on right, even when friends and family believe you are guilty and distance themselves from you. It feels cold and heartless because these are the same people who sat at the table and ate with you. They witnessed how hard you worked and how you kept a paper trail for everything including paper clips. They surely knew these things being said about you in the news are not true because they know your character! Unfortunately, this is the lesson that still haunts me. Be careful who you let in your circle, everyone is not down for you. A hard lesson to learn.

Journal entry: June 14, 2011

When I first started writing my thoughts on what to write were all over the place. I would stop, start, stop and finally words of encouragement from people who said just do it no matter what helped to inspire me to continue. I felt in my soul I had to complete this chapter of my life. In doing so it would help me to complete the full circle of understanding the storm I encountered. This was not an easy task. When those three letters, FBI, come knocking at your door - it is no joke. First, you have no idea why they are there but by the time they finish with the conversation you do have some understanding of the situation. The trial itself kicked my butt. It was no joke by any means. When you go through something this devastating, God is the only one able to bring you through. It makes you crystal clear where you stand. One thing I learned is to always maintain self. Do not try to be anyone else, always keep your own identity. I've learned, when you stand for what you believe in, you are a force to be reckoned with. Walking through the fire will help you to become a positive force and show you how to make things happen for yourself and others. You are the best thing that ever happened. Go through a tough situation and pay attention to who is still rocking with you. Those will be the ones who are loyal to you. Keep them in your circle. There are people that have no character, no integrity and the truth is not in them. A lesson learned.

This book was a healing tool for me because I lived through every *second of it. It was God who gave me the strength to withstand and come out on the other side of his Glory. God put people in my corner to help me understand what was going on. I had to often pause in my footsteps and just stand still and listen to the quiet. God removed so many fake friends, fake family members and those who wanted me to fail. One thing I learned is they can never be me, and I never wanted to be anyone else than who God created me to be.*

During your life's journey you are going to meet people that do not need to be in your space. They may serve a purpose at a particular time, but they are not meant to stay seated at the table. God will place people in our path that you may learn something from the experience. You must pay attention to your space and the energy people bring to your table. Everybody cannot have a front row or back seat in your life. Some people do not deserve the space, because life is precious, you do not have enough time to allow others to waste yours. Once you get these basic little things down, you are half way there.

Journal Entry: June 29, 2011

I have been an entrepreneur since I was 14 years old. I've always wanted to work hard and make a difference in the lives of children. I have been able to continue to make things happen by the Grace of God.

I have had the privilege to do things my way, whether bad, good or indifferent. I have been able to take the good with the bad. I have crossed paths with some remarkable people and had some garbage that needed to be disposed of. The one thing I will always believe is you must delete people out of your circle that do not have your best interest at heart. It is ok to love them from a distance. I have a gift in discernment that had to be developed. When you are focused, and you want something out of life, and you are willing to work hard for it, don't give up.

Do not let anyone try to belittle you or stop you from dreaming big!

When you know what you want, go after it! I am a ghetto chic from Jersey City, New Jersey that has grown to be a woman of substance and character. I am proud and not ashamed of any of the struggles I've been through. I would not trade my life for nothing. Please let's be clear, I did not want to go to prison but I had to fight and believe in myself and my team. People are going to speak against you and support you when everything is good. The people God has put in your life will always support you and will be around through both. Know that what God has for you, is for you. Just because others want to believe what they want, this should not stop your flow. It should help to fuel your drive to succeed.

Journal Entry: June 29, 2011

In starting a new chapter of information through my eyes during this hard journey. I have learned to always keep standing and staying alive, no matter what comes my way. It may have crossed my mind to give up, but it was never an option. I was so hurt and disappointed that so many people, especially the ones that were close to me lost the front row seat in my life. I was angry when someone close to me wore a wire for the FBI trying to coerce answers from me. It was a scene out of law and order. It showed me the real life from the streets and the word snitch is real even when they lie. Family relationships you think you had can go down the drain in a matter of days and both of you have been there for each other since childhood. I was friends with someone for over twenty years and she showed her real character, her real identity, of not being an honest person and not worthy of my friendship. People tend to forget when it's convenient for them. They forget the things they have done in secret that I know about. They forget how much you have covered for them, and they will forget how much they lied directly to your face. What is the sense of having *friends? Then I had over eight months to ponder the question, and I figured out the answer in my stillness. They were only friends for a season and those leaves are often wilted at the end of the trial. Memories locked away but still I must keep it moving. A lesson learned.*

Throughout this book I searched and wrote the answer to how. How I accepted and repented for everything that was for me. I do not blame anyone for anything I experienced. The lessons were for me. The solid personal relationships that I have acquired, you cannot buy. I did learn that God's hand is the orchestra of my life and his hand was on me the entire time. I could not see it of course, but I felt it. When you're in the mist of adversity, it may be hard to know he is still on the throne. He is a healer, a confidant and provides restoration in life, love and business.

This trial kicked my behind. Just for the record, healing takes time. Allow yourself time to feel each emotion through prayer. This is another reason I am adamant about providing our youth opportunities to excel and strive for excellence in education. In writing this book, I wrote what was on my heart, so bear with me as this is my first published manuscript.

Chapter IV

Trial & Testimony

When I began writing this chapter on healing, I knew it would take its toll on me. It was like going to the psychiatrist office and lying on the couch. The only couch I lay on is my own and I know it was God who directed my footsteps and my heart! You never know what you will get when you trust Him. A lesson learned.

When you take the time to listen, he will reveal everything to you within time. I was forty-two years old during the writing of this book. I am proud to say I am in a good place in 2017 as I am preparing to publish this manuscript. It is really a blessing and a gift from God to share some of my experiences on how I, Tamika Riley went to prison and healed from everything the enemy tried to destroy me with.

Who would have thought I would become a published author? I believed it, that's who. To the readers of this book. Please be clear, there were some people that didn't even know me, wished me harm. There were people that stood right next to me that wished I would have went to prison longer than ten months. This shamed me more, because of who they were. I really had to stand quiet and let my healing take place. I am a work in progress. Some people are not even worth the conversation. The lesson is to stay focused and to stay honest to yourself. Do not lose yourself for no one. This journey through the system seemed like it was never going to end, it felt like eternity. Sometimes it felt like a bad dream, and I was not going to wake up. Guess what readers, it was not a dream and I was truly awake. With every second, every minute, every hour, it was all for me. This book is for me to share the lessons that helped me to rise to this next level.

The trial was like being the star in a Broadway production, and going to Alderson Federal Prison was like being on a reality TV show where I was the only one in the audience. The different scenes that played out in the past are over. Thank God! It was His grace and mercy. It was learning and leaning not on my own understanding, but in all my ways I acknowledged Him. Let the kindness of your heart and dedication of your spirit, be acceptable in God's presence through positive focus as love remains brave and without ego.

-Tamika McReynolds-

Today is a new day to share this chapter of what I have learned within the last couple of years. I want to remind people when you learn different things, try to apply it to your life whether it's negative or positive. Every lesson is a teaching experience. Being brave and standing tall no matter what circumstances you are facing. I have learned so much by just watching people. People will reveal themselves eventually, but you have to learn how to listen intuitively. Sometimes when you are slowed down by an illness, or a prison sentence, or any life changing traumatic situation; see who is left in your circle and is genuine in their motives for being in your life. Sometimes I felt lost and betrayed, but through it all I knew I had someone standing by my side. It's weird to explain going from a little girl, to a teenager, a young adult and then a grown woman taking on responsibilities and living life.

Throughout my life and my career, I learned to fight my own battles and not blame anyone else. I learned to take the good with the bad. These different situations and experiences made it a good run. This statement was not always true. When you are going through some mess, you cannot make sense of the struggle. That's why they say; when you don't know, don't ask your man, or your girl, your brother or sister, go straight to the source to get the answers and the truth. Go directly to God!

Writing this book was so helpful and was a true mode of therapy for me. It gave me the opportunity to see the entire situation clearly. I had the time to be still in my thoughts, and it enabled me to be able to talk about it without being bitter. Please understand, I am still angry at times, when an issue arises reminding me of a certain memory, but every day I gain a clearer understanding on my life and how allowing time to heal can change your life. It was intriguing to me at the time, becoming involved personally with a powerful married man. I knew it wasn't cool, but it was a mistake I truly apologize for. When others cast judgment on another that is their problem, not yours.

You and I both know with my mistake I took ownership, it was a learning experience and an unforgettable life moment. I cannot say anything bad regarding the Honorable. He never caused me any harm, but we should not have been in that courtroom. If there was something I did wrong, I will take it all day long but to be accused of something you did not do, that's a problem for me. Others can have their opinions, but to me, if you don't know the facts, sit down and shut up. This book is a depiction of the lessons learned after going through this process. Seeing myself on almost every media outlet, every channel, radio station, including the Spanish Station was surreal. It felt like something out of a movie. It played in real time like a scary horror flick.

Journal Entry: September 25, 2011

We all know what movies and reality TV are, right? It's all for your entertainment, but this was real life. Behind the scenes people are living real life, and for others to receive satisfaction from another's downfall is wrong. As adults, we have a choice on which decisions we make, it's called grown people do grown up things. With this responsibility we must stand on our decisions no matter which way life's journey takes you. We all make mistakes, to become successful we all must learn during the process.

During my trial, it was the most dramatic experience I have ever gone through. It was moving in slow motion, and I could not catch up. It felt like it wasn't going to end. I can't really explain it, but I am going to try my best, so you can read the lesson and learn something from it.

With my brief relationship with the Honorable, it was just a caring and private moment for me. Neither of us tried to or set out to hurt anyone or each other. I can say it was a bad choice to get involved, but it happened, and I take full responsibility for it. I do not regret anything in my life, but I do try to always learn from them. My goal is to become a better person and make wiser decisions in the future. I can't say I am perfect, but I can tell you that I have made steady progress. A lesson learned.

During this nightmare, the trial, I asked a couple of the few friends I had left, "why is this happening to me?" I will never forget my god-brother said to me, "why not you sweetie?" I was stuck, I was speechless, and if you know me, I am never speechless. After that conversation I got it together. My mind, body and soul were ready to fight. It was like God came down from Heaven personally and said, you will get through this because I am in charge! If you know Him like I know Him, this is called walking by faith. Now faith is the substance of things hoped for, and the evidence of things not seen. Believe you will get through the tumultuous times. This trial was to play out the way it was suppose too, I had no control whatsoever, but my team and I did feel we had a say about how long I would go away to prison. Everything happened the way it should have. I did not get this in the beginning, but once I started to understand what was really happening, my brain turned on and my heart turned off. This trial was not about me, but that's what they wanted the public to perceive. Someone once told me, when you know the truth, nothing else matters.

In this book if you do not get anything out of it please get this, when you know the truth, you can stand on it no matter what comes your way. The parties involved in this trial was for show and tell, all I did was show up every day to fight for me. I don't claim I know everything that was going on, as far as the legal terminology, but I got why the hell I was there.

Journal Entry: *October 10, 2011*

Going through a bad situation you must always tune in and listen to that voice within. You must pay attention always. Of course, it's important to have some people that know their profession to give you some sound advice, but when you are spiritually in tune, God will speak directly to your heart! When you go with your intuition things start to unravel. That's the voice inside that I learned to recognize in my healing. The spirit of my Lord and Savior has the last word always. Believe that.

I had to fight for my life no matter what so called friends or the public thought. This was not about them; that part was strictly about me fighting for my rights and my sanity. Now please be clear, I do not wish this bad experience on anyone because in the beginning I did not think I would survive. I thought I was going to die. I thought everything I worked for was coming to an end. I thought everything I accomplished was going down the drain. I felt, how could this happen with so many good things I pride myself on especially when it comes to serving children in my community. Ask yourself what have you done for your community? Like I tell everyone who ask questions, "go catch a case and write your own story." This is my story my way. The people I surround myself with now are not in it just for the ride, they want to actually make a positive difference in the community.

Well, again, that voice in my head, the talk with my creator; it was all as clear as running water. It said, "This situation that you are getting ready to encounter is only for you, Ms. Riley. So, get ready because you are taking this journey." No matter how hard I was trying to make myself think this cannot be happening, but it really is. This was the lesson of a lifetime. You better put your armor on because you are going to need it. The Armor, that is! What are you going through right now? Who are you not feeling comfortable around, and you guys have been rocking for a minute now? I challenge you to switch things up a bit. Go within, be still, pray, and most importantly be quiet! Stop telling everyone your business. Write it down for yourself. Stop seeking the approval of others and validation when it comes to your dreams. Remember you will be the one to renew, recharge, regroup, and readjust and start to move differently.

The trial was the hardest thing I ever went through. The healing was the bravest thing I ever went through. I knew once I got through this, it was going to make me stronger in continuing my life *toward success with my God giving purpose.*

It was such a dark period in my life. I felt like I could not see. I felt at one point, God had left me. My mind was in disarray. I was confused, but somehow, someway, when I could not pray for myself, someone was praying for me. When something like this happened, I started not believing. I cried, I hurt, but after crying, after hurting; in the midst of darkness - I had to stand tall! I even put on some of my 6-7-inch heels, just to be taller! Going to court every day during the trial, I could not show defeat. I had to always remain with myself, within my spirit and my truth. I had to fight even though I had conflicting emotions. Please understand, this was no easy ride for me. It was hard! It was devastating! It was the darkest times and I thought I would never see light again. God sent me an Angel to remind me about FAITH.

Let's be clear, I do not claim like I know the Bible inside out, because I don't. I can say I know that God carried me and sent me help in my time of need. He is a comforter. What area of your life do you need God to comfort you? Walk in his will while you are in the storm of life, not only when everything is all good. Establish your foundation in the Word of God and when trouble arises for whatever situation you are in, you can stand on that to draw knowledge and understanding from a universal perspective. A higher power.

Journal Entry: *October 24, 2011*

To save my life that higher power sent me everything I needed to get through the trial of 2008. Even though I went to trial, and even though I did go to prison; I fought for me with the best team in the world, sent by God! Krovatin and the dream team! When I finally got a grip on things and began removing toxic people from the space of my life, all while going through the trial, my world started falling into God's plan for my life to move in his divine order. Again, the lessons were for me, but the trial was not!

I guess I can say I needed this lesson, so I would be able to share my life experiences to help someone else. I know God placed me here for a purpose. All of us have a purpose; we have to get in tune to find it. Internally is the only place you will find the passion and drive to move forward. Open your heart to him, and watch you become at peace when all hell is breaking out around you.

I am sure by now; some people have read about my story online, the newspapers, on TV, or followed my case. Some sound advice; do not believe everything you read in the newspapers or see on Television. The trial, seemed like it was the only news on all the media in my city. It was like the reporters were not seeing anything else in the world. One word; distractions. Every time I turned around, it seemed like everything was Tamika Riley. All I said; was why? But, I keep hearing my god brothers voice; "why not you?" I got it.

Each time I begin to write, it felt like the very first time. A new word always came to my mind and spirit that I believed wholeheartedly. After reviewing several chapters in completing this book, the main lesson is clear for me; it is to stay in the moment and use my life to teach someone else. That is something I heard from the Oprah Winfrey show years ago.

This book is such a healing device for me, I thank God for putting it on my heart to write my feelings on paper while I was going through everything. You will feel hurt and anger, but also positive lessons you can apply to your life. I cannot tell you that you will not go through certain emotions, but I can tell you that you will come out victorious.

I am so grateful that I am here to present this experience my way and hope others will learn something from it. One thing that comes to mind, is to use your life's journey to learn as you go. Stay focused no matter how bad it gets. This life's journey is about the good, bad and how you use the tools you've earned to keep it moving. Heal-

ing from the trial was so much for me. Not just dealing with the Honorable, but people I never met wished me harm. It was also surreal how people in this world are so unhappy, they wish negativity on others. Again, this is why you have to stay prayed up and continue to go after your dreams. In this world things are going to happen. What you need to know is how to deal with them, mentally, and spiritually or it can affect you physically.

Healing through this process has made me a stronger and wiser person. I did not know anything about the law or my rights, but I learned quickly. Being in such a high-profile case was unforgettable, and it seemed like the flashlights were never coming back on. I am so happy I had a few friends that used their own flashlights so I could see. They guided the way until the lights came back on; it was the beginning for me in understanding character and integrity.

This book is just like an interview. I'm just trying to cover the facts, the hurt and the healing. So many things I wanted to talk about, but I had to narrow the events to my experience of coming through a storm and the lessons learned. This should give you a sense of what happened to me and how I went to prison for having an affair with a powerful, high-profile, married man. The trial in 2008 was surrounded by a political figure that never did any harm to me, so how the hell did I get here? Your guess is as good as mine.

My interpretation with the FBI was not clear. It took a minute before my blinders were removed. Even today I am still asking the question internally, why?

So, let's move on to the part about me getting indicted. After being indicted, I made the decision that it would be better if we went to trial. This was the best way for me to fight for me. So now, I'm going to court every day listening to people say things that are not true. I couldn't understand it, but I snapped out of the shock understanding why these things are happening. I am in public relations, so I am clear when you read the made-up stories to help sell newspapers and boost TV ratings. I got the message. On the reverse, the message I want to send is; I will not take the blame for something I did not do. Like my Attorney

Gerry would say; "it's one thing to lay down when you do something wrong but what happens when you know in your heart you did not do what you are being accused of?" That is when you need to stand up for yourself, no matter what anyone is thinking or saying! I have never been a follower and never will be. I wasn't raised that way. I am not the type of person to be persuaded into doing wrong; although with the allegations I felt confident my paper trail on all dealings would stand up. Negative - that didn't happen! A lesson learned.

Now please understand, I did not want to go to prison but I had to fight for my life. What are you going through that you feel like you may not make it? That you may not come out a winner? You must believe you are the winner already. That is where you start.

It wasn't easy going to court every day, just waiting through the process. The main goal of the prosecution was an eye for an eye, anything for political gain, and I was caught in the crossfire and found guilty. Yes, I was asked to wear a wire on the Mayor and I refused. DID NOT WEAR THE WIRE - END OF STORY!!!!

After being convicted, I was like, are you kidding me? This can't be real. Guess what diva, it's real and you must deal with the cards you have been dealt. Now for sentencing, on how much time I will get in prison. I was sentenced to ten months. I could not wait until I could check in. I could not wait to start my time, because then, I knew it would be over. This moment in history will be a part of my past. A lesson learned.

These are lessons of a lifetime. Lessons you will never forget as long as you live. So many lessons we can learn from these positive words, I kept close to my heart and I wanted to share.

Standing with God

Fight

Truth

Character

Favor

Faith

Chapter V

Release & Integrity

Arriving at camp cupcake, I tried to check in early, but I could not. I did arrive in Alderson, West Virginia to the prison camp after 5:00 AM to start my time. I drove myself to Virginia the day before to pick up both my girls, Ree (Arthuree Lawrence) and Cham (Francine Dawkins) who rode with me, as I drove myself to prison on a chilly sunny, Sunday morning. This was such a relief, I felt the worst part was over. This is exactly how it was supposed to happen, all that's left now is to take the ride. I tried to mentally prepare for intake before the actual moment of entering the prison. I felt this would help me learn from the experience. No one wants to go to prison. I can't speak for anyone else, but for me, Tamika Riley, did not want to go to prison!

Journal Entry: *October 25, 2011*

Picking up the pieces and referencing this manuscript, has become the opportunity of a lifetime. This experience has made me grow into a forgiving person who still has a way to go. I am still a work in progress. It has also made me really understand people. One factor I know for sure; everybody does not think like you, and everyone does not have the same values as you. Apply it to your home life, your career and your business associates. This is a hard lesson to learn.

This book traveled miles with me and has led me to really understand life. We must understand that things happen whether it is good or bad. What I know for sure is; we have one and it can only be changed by you. Stand on right and what you believe in. I am at peace through this mess, I thank God for my mother and father, for the night they made Tamika Riley! Truly I am a woman who is humbled and proud of whom I am no matter what the circumstances may be. Being in Federal Court everyday was no joke and going to Alderson prison was no joke.

What I learned made me stronger and wiser in really learning how to interpret the word Faith and apply it to the circumstances I was dealing with internally. I must say, these lessons have been footprints for my life. I do not mind passing it along. Especially if a young person can apply it to their everyday life. Sometimes I had the thought it may be too late to complete the book, no one will probably read it. Then I snapped out of it and realized the goal is for me to complete it, and the message is for someone else to receive it. This is how your soul is able to let go of the hurt and pain and start to heal.

Journal Entry: November 4, 2011

During my brief affair with the Honorable, it was a valuable lesson that replays sometimes in my thoughts. Sometimes we make choices I feel we can learn from. I don't use the word regret in the decisions that I have chosen for me, but I do use them as a growth mechanism to not do it again, especially if it was detrimental to others and myself. The people that have entered my space had been a real-world spin, I enjoyed the lessons they taught me. It was so difficult going to prison, but it built me into a virtuous woman. This experience taught me that people are truly full of it and I must keep it moving. Before I was able to wrap my head around dishonesty, I was on my way to the same place where Martha served her prison sentence. Look at her now, she is on a hit show with Snoop Dogg. Don't tell me what the power of God won't do. God believes in second chances and so do I. This lesson did help me began to understand the system, politics and political gain. One bit of advice I would like to offer from this experience is; don't stand for bull. If you know you are right, fight until the end.

One of my stepsons always used to say, "Make them kill you". I used to look at him like he was crazy, but then I got it! Being accused of something you did not do is a hard pill to swallow. Going through the fire, refusing to bow down to man; know that God is your fire extinguisher. He will walk with you through the fire, but you must get in the heat and hold it steady until the flames die down around you. Just *don't give up!*

This book is full of lessons but one thing I want young people to remember is to stay honest. Character is very important. Don't get off the focus train because sometimes when you follow others, you will forget the truth about yourself. Listen to your gut; listen to that voice speaking to you because you cannot lose.

The prison stay close to ten months, was a real cleansing for me. Not being able to go where you want, see your family when you want, buy Dunkin Donuts coffee at Bayonne Line, purchasing 6-inch stilettos or even taking a nice ride on the highway. Your freedom is gone, and you have to listen to others tell you when to eat, sleep and read, It's an eye opener. Please do not be disillusioned, prison is a place you don't want to be. Don't let people tell you otherwise. The difference is, if you did not do what someone is accusing you of, tell them to tell your story while walking because you will fight for your rights. Prison did something different to me. It made me realize my worth on a higher level.

Journal Entry: *November 5, 2011*

Being by myself really made me think about how God really blesses me in helping others, especially, young people. It made me believe no matter what you're going through, know you are to create a space.

Going to Alderson, West Virginia happened so fast, it was like a roller coaster that would not stop.

Walk with me as I list a few more lessons:

- *Fight for your freedom*

- *Determination is within*

- *Stand in the mist of adversity*

- *Validation is free*

- *Complete what you started*

- *Finish with integrity*

- *Motivate others from your journey*

I hope the readers can really relate to the lessons at hand. I am so grateful of my space and my being. I acknowledge my faults, my mistakes and have asked God to show me the way. I recognize that negative people have a job to do. There are some miserable people in this world with their own negative being. Do not allow them to be in your space. Tell them to keep it moving. This whole ordeal was devastating, destructive, and a complete nightmare, but guess who is still here running her mouth?

Journal Entry: *December 12, 2011*

The media, the press, the newspapers, and the Spanish channel covered my trial. People were chit-chatting like they were in the courtroom. If you are going to talk; talk about what you know. That's the lesson!

Find your own way for you, not for anyone else. You have to apply the lessons to your life. Indulge in your experience, embrace the rescue. What do I mean? When you get your emotions in sync at that moment it brings you back to a place of positive energy surrounding you. I never thought of myself as being invisible. What others thought of me didn't matter, I knew it! My mom and dad taught me that I matter, no matter what others think or say. My self-esteem has been on next level status since childhood from the teachings of my mother. She stood her ground always and let my brother and I know we can reach for the stars in life. Melting into this case, those values went into action.

Being true to self, having good character, and knowing how to carve out your space in the world are the keys to winning in life. Know it in your heart, believe in your own determination, and don't show any fear. Those instincts went into gear automatically. It was like I turned into a superhero, my own Tamika badass, as I connected with my Inner soul and visited that place within that was strong and confident. This is the place I always want my spirit to reside... in peace, knowing who I am. This is where I am going and want to stay. That moment is living in the moment. That time is now.

During my prison sentence, I had time to reflect on everything. I felt betrayed; I felt hurt that was unimaginable. I felt there were people who really showed their true colors, but most importantly I had to learn this lesson all by myself. God's lesson was for me only, but this book is for me to share with you.

Once I started to embrace the facts after speaking with my Attorney Gerry Krovatin, he was one of my greatest teachers. Man, did he teach me some things. So many of the questions I needed answers to, he was able to answer. When I first sat with Jerry, I felt he did not feel what I was saying, or he wasn't listening to me. I felt he thought I was just another criminal to him but that changed in a flash. When you know the truth, it does reveal itself. My Attorney had to come back to me and say he made a mistake and that he believed me. That makes a huge difference. You know you are caught up in some mess, when the law team representing you believes you like they believed in me, the dynamics of the situation changes. The trial made me tough, tender, and mature. With these lessons of going to trial, going to prison; two things can happen, you're going to fight for you or quit on you. If you know your truth, then you will learn a lesson in the fight. Don't settle, *don't settle.*

Walking through the fire helped me so much. This is what I know, not what someone told me, I felt it, I went through. I experienced it firsthand.

Journal Entry: *December 20, 2011*

   It is very important to know what your mistakes are and to grow from there. You don't have to keep giving power to a situation, but you do need to make peace with all things.

   It is also a good lesson to learn from the past because it will assist on how you move in the future.

   One thing I will always remember is too never let people dictate your being. No matter what they say or how they act, do not let negative people in your camp. They will always reveal themselves. It does not matter who they are, friends, relatives, wives, husbands, brothers, cousins, sisters, fathers, or even the next-door neighbor. Some people are not who they claim to be. You must be on guard to protect yourself. Getting into some mess is always hard to get out. If you avoid it and are not preparing to fight, there could be devastating consequences, mainly if you did nothing wrong.

   Please pay attention to your surroundings at all times because that's when enemies try to sneak up on you! I do not believe in keeping your enemies closer. Never have. I am good, stay away from me and I will stay away from you!

   This book has allowed me to finish the chapter of my life that needed closure. It allowed for more positive things to come into play. I am so grateful that God put it on me to do this and not worry about what people think or say, especially the ones that aren't doing anything or going anywhere. They just talk to be talking. You cannot let what people say about who you are as a person, have any effect on you.

You were born with a set of unique individual gifts and talents. These things help you navigate the world around you. It's where your purpose comes from, that thing way deep on the inside that says, I could do this for free because I love it! The only thing you will give up becoming successful and following your dreams, is your time.

Journal Entry: December 22, 2011

How can you reach your full potential in life while life is still happening around you and others who don't know you try at ever interval to tear down your character and possibly take your freedom, your family and your possessions? The word I meditate on is STAND! You have to stand in the mist of adversity knowing your truth. Forgive yourself for any mistakes made. It will be up to you to find out where you went wrong and how you're going to come out on the winning end. Your victory must first start in your mind. Focus on overcoming the difficulties that can alter your direction. Your walk-through life will not be perfect by any means. It is all balls down to your mental state in every situation that determines your individual outcome.

The key to a fulfilled life:

Follow your Destiny and those things you are passionate about

Your Strength comes from within

Move forward but always put God first

What you think about yourself will determine your outcome

Despite it all you can live harmoniously

Journal Entry: December 27, 2011

The words that come to mind today is... Thank You.

> *The things I have learned about my own heart beat and wondering when the pain would stop. Let me explain, I put my pain into writing. I started this book then stopped. I picked it up again and set it down just as some of you are doing with situations and dreams in your life. We are our own worst enemy. Nothing is holding you back from writing a book or creating that business or slaying those grades in the classroom but fear and FEAR alone. Why do you think kids are bullied in school? It's to inject fear, but God said to fear no one but him. Why do you think that is? It's because God knew bullies would exist, right? It seems to start at a very young age. Think about the mentality of a young bully. Where is this anger, this need to control another person or to have power over another, come from? Again, FEAR and fear alone. Someone who takes advantage of someone they deem to be lesser than they are is called a bully. Their job is to keep you in bondage, thinking of the situation day and night. It will paralyze you from moving forward, from going outside, from hanging out with friends and from becoming the amazing young person that you are! Read your Bible for yourself, in your room, in your quiet time. Then you will soon know, you are the head and not the tail. Your life matters, you have dreams and goals that you can do right now! Do not let fear hold you back from doing anything. Control your thoughts by feeding it positive affirmations daily. It's important for me to tell young people, the way you think about yourself is the only jail free card you will receive from me. Speak up for yourself without fighting and killing. Have a battle on the mic through writing poetry, hip-hop or dance to express positive change in your inner circle and your community.*

> *I know it is important to complete what you start and not be afraid of who you are. The book has been a tool for me to keep moving with all the lessons that have come my way!*

When you go through rocky situations that can cause turmoil, you have to make up your mind to fight and not to give up. With this 2nd chance of my life I want to dedicate this book to our youth. I want to continue to give back. This is my life. This is a part of who I am. The trial tried to destroy my being. It tried to destroy my meaning, but I thank God for not taking me away. As each day goes by and this manuscript is not completed, I go back and check myself and realize this book is not just about me, it is for someone else! Sometimes, I ask myself what are you thinking when it comes to writing this book? I thought "who are you to write a book?" I said to myself... "I am just a ghetto chick from Jersey City, just trying to help someone reach their full potential and in doing that I free myself each and every time". My book has inspired me even when it was not completed as I was able to go back and tell myself; "Tamika you must finish this no matter what. Writing these chapters has inspired me to finish what I started. Writing a book is something most people are afraid to do. Telling my story made me believe I can help others through sharing the lessons I've learned. I pray these chapters can relate to all those that have been through some mess and did not know what in the hell had hit them. This too shall pass, just stay humble and free of fear.

It's one thing to give some lessons, it is another if you actually get the lesson. You must learn what goes around comes around. It's called KARMA!!! You will be the only one to know. Don't let others define your narrative. They did not give it to you and they cannot take it from you. Once you learn your journey is yours, you will be open to all the possibilities life has to offer, because we each have a purpose. Will you let your purpose die with you? Or will you at least try to live out your purpose? Try it and see. Once you know your enemies (fear), then channel it, you will find your meaning and you will know your purpose.

Journal Entry: *January 2, 2012*

   Writing this book forced me to define its purpose. The definition or description I offer to chapters within is the unveiling. An unveiling of me and my defining journey. To define the life changing moments of Tamika! I am so happy to say with all the darkness God gave me, doors he left to be opened for me to continue to make a difference. It has allowed me to open the next chapter of my life and I am HAPPY to take the walk through the door to go through my journey. I plan on opening that same door for young ladies coming behind me. Always learn from your mistakes, take an internal look daily to cleanse your spirit and walk in your God giving gifts and talents.

   The book has been a rebirth and the moment is for me. This is my moment because during the trial everyone had noise makers like at a New Year's Eve Party! What the Hell!

   I have not spoken publicly to any media outlet or magazine about my case with the Mayor of Newark NJ, The Honorable Sharpe James. I did not read the headlines. I did not react, but I connected to myself. I know what it takes to sell papers- boost ratings. Well, now it's my turn to speak and hope our youth will get something out of it!

   The question that comes to my mind often is; who or what made me want to write a book about the trials and tribulations of my life? Well, one day I picked up a notebook because I needed an outlet to release some of the tension from the trial. By the time I looked up, I was in prison and it was three notebooks later. After I came home from prison it was six notebooks later and two were five subjects. I wanted this book to remain the same as Inspirational Letters from Tamika, so the youth had a daily playbook of lessons learned and how to stay positive and work through your emotions when dealing with adversity. I went through every emotion, from sadness to mostly anger. I was angry at fake friends who I felt no longer supported me, we had been friends for over twenty-five years. I had family members turn their

71

backs on me like I did something to them and they know my character. I noticed the trial did take a toll on me, but my heart has always been about friends and family. Anyone who knows me will tell you this is the absolute truth. So, a lot of my anger came from being hurt by friends and family and the repercussions of their actions.

Journal Entry: January 4, 2012

Well so much has happened, and I am making sure I have it all together. I hope and pray someone will be able to learn from this ordeal. It is such a privilege to be able to write my story, in my own design. So much has happened it keeps getting better and better.

One thing I did not know that would happen, was me learning how to forgive. Sometimes you forget to forgive and just try to keep it moving. Let's not be anyone's fool, you will always have to be on your guard when it comes to haters. Sometimes, you have to do what you have to do.

Chapter VI

Redemption & Favor

I have been so side tracked having my book be in a pending stage. I also think about TI the rapper, regarding his strength with his wife and family, that keep it moving no matter what the situation is. Sometimes, going through your own situations, you really have time to reflect and say it's time to complete what you have started hearing.

Journal Entry: *May 12, 2012*

Who does that? Who stands by you when you get in trouble? Who stands by you when you go to prison? Let me hurry up and answer... My husband and my daddy. There are some others, Cham, Ree and Mother Mason that stood tall and never turned their backs on me. I kept saying to myself even when I thought I lost my edge, God gave me my insight to finish. It's hard when you try to put everything together regarding a bad situation that has turned into God's blessing!

Stopped in my tracks - why this is not finished? Diva, the answer was it was not time. To everyone who reads this book, I hope you will enjoy at least one thing if not the whole thing.

One thing I have learned while writing this book, do not stop going after your dreams. Prison taught me so much about my life. I truly missed my family and the few friends I left behind. I thought sometimes a while back, I would not finish this project. Don't ask why, but I must thank the FBI for making me stronger.

After being in a major case with the Honorable, who would have thought you can make it after the cameras, press, including the Spanish stations. During the trial with the Honorable, it was a damn life changing event!

When the FBI came to my residence, first thing I was thinking is, they have the wrong address. After you verify you are the person they are looking for, your whole mindset changes.

It seems to me until you go through something dark like the trial of 2008, you have no idea what you are made of. Catching a high-profile case is not a joke at all. This will either break you or make you. During this time, I truly learned about me and who I was fighting for. No matter how many cameras, reporters, liars, government officials, fake friends, I was able to see the bull that was in front of me. This gave me such an inner peace that I cannot explain.

My case with the Honorable was an unforgettable time for me. During these hard times, the truth was not present, and I did not understand the law. I did not understand how people can come into a Federal Courtroom and put their hands on the Bible and just lie! I then snapped out of it and took it for what it was worth.

Journal Entry: May 26, 2012

This book is about different challenges and tribulations I had to go through. My trial in 2007-2008, was the worst thing I ever had to experience. This trial helped define who and what was worth fighting for. My case was talked about like nothing else mattered in the world. I couldn't put my finger on it, but I know every time I turned on the tv, or saw the newspaper, my name was everywhere - go figure.

Before catching my case, I was a force to be reckoned with that God placed here for a reason. I have been blessed to be in the position for the last 20 years to help others no matter what. My career path has made me the person that I am very proud to be. My dad and Mom are truly gifts from God that instilled purpose and substance for my life. They taught me, never to give up and to go after my dreams.

With this, it helped to build me into the woman I have become, and I am always trying to be the best I can be.

The people that know me, Tamika Riley, really know me and who I am. I cannot sell that or make you know me. You either do or you don't. Saying this helps me to rally and know I love the woman I have become. I love that, I just didn't begin to help others. This characteristic is my DNA, it is who I am. I cannot say that for some of the people that were allowed in my life. During my trial, I really found some things out about my so-called friends or people that think they are dream makers. Who in the world designated themselves as a dream maker? I ask this because they are not truthful about their own lives? The funny thing is, people will try to be something they are not.

With the different companies I had the pleasure and oppor-tunity to work for, I learned so many things and one thing I can't forget is the truth.

During my journey, I know for me, my heart truly loved the Mayor and respected him. I have said it over and over, he never did anything illegal with me. He never did anything to hurt me. He was a loving and kind man that I was blessed to have in my life for a short period of time. He taught me so much about life, and always respected me as a woman trying to make a difference. My relationship with a married man is not cool, but I did it, and I am very sorry for the pain I have caused. My feelings for the Mayor were clear, he was a good per-son and was always willing to help millions of people.

My brief but sacred moments with the Honorable were very meaningful to me. When the news hit that I was his brief girlfriend, I took that with dignity because I know in my heart what I meant to him. I never had set out to hurt anyone. The feelings for him you can't turn them off and on. It was what it was, if only for a moment.

The one thing I really want to be clear about is, we should not have been in that courtroom for those charges. I have made some mis-takes in my life but being indicted, that was a problem.

Sometimes decisions are made, and I am a true believer about consequences. My love for the Honorable held up because I know why I was there. Not in the beginning, but then God revealed it to me and that's why I decided to fight for my life. In life we make decisions with relationships and you never know how things are going to turn out, but I must say I never wish anyone any harm.

My lessons during my relationship with the Honorable were, I respected the table. I will always treasure the moments I had with him, it was truly a learning experience.

During the trial; when everyone wanted to speak about something regarding my relationship with the Mayor, a person they did not know. It was very hurtful, when people are just being negative. But I got over it really quick, because I know the truth.

One thing I know for sure is when you love a person, no one else can stand and speak on your behalf. My relationship with the Honorable was a private and personal decision that I made, was it the best, no but I will stand on it. No one can tell you who to love.

People often ask, why didn't you just lie on the Mayor? My answer is, that's not who I am. DAMN IT, I WOULD NOT WANT NO ONE TO LIE ON ME, LIKE THEY DID AT THE TRIAL...

Please, let's not be confused, I was very angry for being there, but he had done nothing to me.

When you go through something like our 2008 case, you find out who you are in every dimension. One thing I can honestly say, is I really admire the Mayor for the man he was to me. Again, I say this for the record, and you are hearing directly from me. The Honorable never did anything illegal with me! Did you get that? Movement is everything! Cover that in the media!!!

From Federal Prison To First Lady

Chapter VII

Forgiveness & Mercy

I remember the tears could not stop, no matter how much tissue I gathered. The tears would keep flowing. One day my Pastor made a call to Mother Mason and I had to get on the phone. Mother Mason is a spirit filled woman who came into my life as an elder with the wisdom and knowledge I needed. She helped me transition into being the First Lady of Mt. Olive Baptist Church. I remember the words of encouragement that God would use this mother of the church to speak guidance into me. Mother Mason, a woman of faith and substance would guide me as a woman with her sound board of sacred messages sent especially for me. This is the divine way in which women can always support each other.

Once I realized why the tears would not stop. I started piecing the puzzle together. I could not believe all the things that were happening, and people claiming to love me were trying to hurt me. This was a light bulb that went off in my head. When you know the truth, keep it moving, and stand on what you believe.

The tears that came from my eyes were all the fake friendships pouring cement over healing wounds, once I got it, the tears stopped flowing and lay rock solid in earth. The pain caused by my trial was a life changing experience that I did not think I was coming out of. The pain and the fears that were caused by this darkness helped me keep it together. It allowed me to be scared but understand the dynamic of the situation. Once I was able to break it down, everything started clicking on what really was happening to me; a black woman.

I learned it is ok to cry and get it out of my system, but once the tears stopped, I looked up and started kicking butt.

If you are a strong seasoned woman, you should have a younger woman by your side to guide and push forward through this world we live in. Who do you think is best to have advice from, to help you move through these trying times? You see women making an impact in every aspect of society, in every part of the globe. We are powerful alone, but with the right vibrations of powerful women before us, beside us, leading and encouraging us, we are a force to be recognized.

We deserve equality and respect as we do the work, and we

should be compensated magnificently for it. Women are called everything in the book when we speak our minds or say, "no I am not going
to be able to do that." It is ok to say you do not understand when you
are not comfortable with a situation you are in. It does not mean you
know what to do, or how to maneuver away from the negativity. It
simply means you acknowledge a lack of understanding. Let me be
clear, that does not mean you don't research and ask questions to find
out how you can fight for yourself. Women are very resourceful crea-
tures. Women bare children, work, take care of home, cook, run major
corporations, operate small businesses from home or online, and they
are writing and blogging about life experience from a woman's perspective.

I may have physically spent time in prison, but my mind was
always strong even when I could not feel it. Some women are mentally
in prison and have never stepped a foot in the building. I am here to
tell you that your struggle is not in vain. Keep doing and guiding younger women on this journey called life. She needs assistance with going
to school, avoiding drugs, alcohol, physical abuse (in and out of the
home), raising children, going back to school, feeding herself and her
babies, having self-love and not letting others take advantage of her
kindness. Women are worthy enough, smart enough, have proven we
are talented enough in handling our business. We have fought for
equal rights and equal pay for what we bring to the table each day. If
you cut any corners anywhere unknowingly, you will be sought after,
interrogated and mislead. Please be very careful, women of color especially. The way to a powerful man is usually through a powerful woman. Always be your own person and fight for who you are, not for anyone else. You will know people by the way they treat you.

When you are on trial in your home state, it seems like the press will never stop talking about you. With all the good we have done I never received the press coverage. There wasn't press coverage when we were helping someone to finish school, staying off drugs, or paying someone tuition, or even using my own funds to purchase turkeys and food for others on Holidays or giving out Christmas toys. My community service has always been top priority. I have been participating in jails in Hudson County since the 90s to empower women, letting them know I cared about each one of them. If it was just to provide hair and makeup or teach them how to dress for an interview. I never thought I would be on the other end years later. I had no agenda to hurt anyone or do anything illegal but having an affair with a married, well-known powerful man, the city stopped; go figure. I wonder if I was of a different race would they have asked me to wear a wire. I am not sure what I was to snitch on, but I passed and the next thing I know, I was indicted along with the Mayor of Newark NJ.

That is the nature of the beast. I must say when you know the truth, you don't care or pay any attention, especially when you know your truth. I am so blessed I had the opportunity to do (public relations), to know how it works in the media world. I am so happy I did not allow them to break me down with their lies. The press knows their job, which was to try to destroy my character. But they did not have the power. I wasn't going to give them the satisfaction. I am glad I was able to keep some reporters employed.

Things I noticed came from the left to the right, but I stayed prayed up. For all the things they reported, I say thanks for spelling my name right. Tamika Riley!

In the case, you had people that wanted to be stars for the day on somebody else's watch. They did not have enough fake news of storytelling about themselves. When you know what you know, it does not matter what anyone writes in papers, in a blog, or gossips out loud.

The media is so messed up in our society but let them do what they do and I am going to keep it moving. Always be ready for the unknown.

The ownership of Tamika Riley, I would not trade my life for the world. This life experience has really taught me something that you can't buy. The experiences of this situation pushed me to the limit. I was changed forever by that experience. I don't trust as much, and I am very particular who comes in my circle. There are already warning signs that get ignored. Something someone said that didn't settle right in your spirit. Underlying jealousy that someone close feels toward you. This is a recipe for disaster because others do not like seeing you excel and will try to tear you down at every angle. You cannot worry about them, but you do have to be aware they are there.

This experience did something to me, way down within myself in which I can't express the feeling at this time. The only way to describe it is complete devastation on a level you can't even imagine. It was such a dark place, I see why some people snap. When you feel like you lost everything and there are people trying to take your life. You gain superhuman internal strength because now you know, you must fight for you. You cannot allow people to think they are in position to take your life, you must learn to hold your own and keep it moving. The ownership of my life comes with all the good and the bad no matter what the circumstances are. Stay focused on what's right. My life has truly been a blessing to share with others. What is your worth? Do you know? How do you figure that out? I wanted to add note sections throughout this book for you to jot down how to learn the lesson through journaling. My notebooks turned into a book. It was healing to express what I was feeling while going to trial and while in prison. I even continued once I was out of prison. Don't ever stop pursuing your dreams. It is never too late. I am publishing this book 10 years later than it was written. It's all in Gods timing. You just have to do the work. Set the date and execute your dreams. Your gifts are vibrant, grand and priceless. Continue to do the research and invest money into your plans. Young people are becoming entrepreneur at 16 years of age and younger.

During this media circus I realized my worth. I know for a fact, I am trying to be the best person I can be, no matter what the haters want to portray. I know who I am, and I have a purpose here on this earth.

The ownership of my life had to endure the 2008 trial of the year because it gave me something you cannot buy at the store. It gave me courage, gave me self-respect, it gave me wisdom, and finally it truly restored my faith. Owning your life means you are in charge. It means that you get to be the producer, the director, the editor, and the writer. It shows, you have the script in your hands and whatever may come your way, you can rewrite, delete or start over. I continue to start over, as I continue to discover other areas and other gifts God had led an open path to.

That's the beauty of trouble coming your way. You have the ability to fight for you. The trouble that came my way was a dark period, but every dark period is not a dead end, period.

Journal Entry: July 27, 2012

Ownership is so important, it helps to guide you in the direction you want your life to go. Owning up to mistakes, fears, and bad decisions are a process of growth. You have an opportunity to make changes. You are in charge of you. No one can make you do anything you don't want to do. All the decisions bad or good, I stand on them. No one forced me to do anything. I am a person of character and integrity that will fight for what's right pertaining to me. Owning up to things you may have done that is not pleasing in God's sight is a hard pill to swallow, but it must be done. Confess with your mouth and ask God for forgivingness. Forgiveness is for you, not the other person.

Being a grown-up takes a lot of drive, value, character and self-love. You have the manuscript. Let the life experiences you encounter help to guide you. You will know when you get this uneasy feeling when something is not right, and you ignore it. Life is short, own it while you can, even with the bad stuff that comes your way. Stay alert, stay honest, and keep the faith. This is a true statement, you only get one shot. You have one life, own it, and respect it!

The lessons I have had the privilege in getting, no matter how much good you do when something bad comes your way, they will try to make all the good go out the window. Well let me tell you a story, when you work hard, you must fight for your worth. People did not give me anything, I worked hard since I was 12 years old. My parents instilled in me certain values and not to give up no matter what.

This life is an honor to have because when you know you are doing the right thing it comes easy. The lessons have not only been both good and bad but better. I cannot complain, even though the hardest lessons of friendship showed me that people are not worth being in your space. But then I realized, everything happens for a reason. You may not understand at that time on how people can betray you like it's nothing, but the Lord knows I know better. People will teach you something and please pay attention to what they show you!

Different lessons will help mold you into the person you will become. I really thank God, for the darkest period I experienced with the Honorable.

My lesson with the Honorable was worth it because God showed me who was in charge. I thank him for not folding, leaving me alone or even giving up on me. The lesson with my trial made me strong and willing to fight for my life. The lessons of standing up for your rights come with strength and dignity. One thing I did learn from my parents was how to fight for you when everyone else gives up on you. Going to trial every day, I can count the people that called to check on me or to see if I needed a bottle of water. They all disappeared, and the phone calls stopped coming. But when I was buying cars, homes and giving out funds, the phone did not stop ringing. To the people that were in my life, I just wanted to say thank you for deleting yourself from my space. Thank you! Thank you! Thank you!

Another lesson I learned through this experience, is not to let people steer you in the wrong direction. Do not be a follower, be a leader. Lead your own path and own it. Take it with the good and the bad. Getting to the root of fear, you have to learn it's normal to feel afraid, but you cannot stay stuck in that space of fear.

Fear will stop you from living and fighting for your rights. I understood, fear was not for me. I had to get a grip of fear and turn that energy into something positive. Fear can kill you or keep you in a place on stillness and you cannot move forward. I did not do what they were proclaiming, so I was able to get real clear, real quick. A tough lesson I learned is when everyone around you gives up on you. When they turn the other way as if they do not see you. They believed exactly what they said in the newspapers; you do not give up at all on yourself, no matter what haters say. Never let fear stop you from living the life you seek. Fear is, fake evidence appearing real. If you give it power, it can leave you in a place of impatience with very low vibrations. We can all control fear from our ego. Dig deep within yourself and change those things within that binds up your emotions in fear. It will stifle your growth in negative thinking and doubt.

Your DNA really shows up and shows you what you are made of. When it is time to be quiet do it, when it's time to be still do that, but when it's time to fight with your knowledge - you must fight.

I heard something from Tyler Perry on TV. It goes something like this;

People throw dirt on you, but they also throw dirt on your casket. I am paraphrasing his message, but I understand the message. Keep it moving and keep God by your side as you move. Fear will paralyze you from reaching your full potential. It will keep you from a new job, a great school, a new small business, and a new home. Fear is something we all have struggled with one way or the other. Once you realize that fear is fear, it cannot hold you back from your dreams. It's just a word. It has no power, until you give it power. You give it power by thinking something bad will take place when it has not happened yet; false evidence appearing real. If I continued to fear the situation, I would have probably given up a long time ago. Becoming fearless takes work and consistent belief in God and yourself. Changing your behavior to defeat self-doubt and fear is a lesson within itself. Face your fears head on by writing them down and bringing them to the surface as visuals will help you to see fear as powerless.

Changing your mind set to think positive thoughts is challenging to say the least. It requires you to be open with yourself and be brutally honest about who you are. Change comes from within. We all go through challenges and trials. Your character and will power should reach higher heights and deeper depths through adversity. Your thinking can directly affect the outcome for the rest of your life.

Chapter VIII

Vindication & Love

Journal Entry: *August 24, 2012*

I have not written in a while to complete my thank you letters. My mind has taken off and been distracted. Why? I can't answer that, but I do know I must complete this mission that has been placed on my heart. It seems right when you are in the mist of completing a special project, things get in the way, but my strength keeps telling me I must complete this mission in order to move on.

Thank You Letters:

Lessons Learned, Lessons Taught

Once you start something in life, you must finish it no matter what. I am so behind with this book but just think Diva, you never wrote a book before. It's your story so do it the way God is planning it out for you. I am so nervous of this completion. It has to be printed no matter what.

This part of the book is very important to me because these are thank you letters to the people I love, and those who was there for me and during the dark period of my life.

I would like to include in this journal entry a few letters of thank you. Let's begin with my husband; Pastor John H McReynolds, he is such a strong man. God lead him to me! God knew what he was doing because I didn't. I want to thank my husband for his belief in me no matter what the news said. He stood by me even when he was getting the gossip on his phone every day. He never judged me. He never talked about me. He never gave up on me. I thank you babe, for being there and standing strong. It amazes me how someone could come into my life and cheer for me more than people who have known me all my life. You kept me strong during and after the trial. Your special cards had everyone in the fish tank excited to sit and read your words of encouragement. It made a difference, not only in my life but others as well. You are a true man who saw my heart, and for that I knew it would be an honor to be your wife. Thank you for praying for me when I did not know how to pray for myself. Rev, I am proud to be your wife, because by any means you are no punk! Thank you! Thank you! Thank you! My thoughts are coming to an end. I think I can finally put this to rest. The past is the past and it can no longer hurt me. One point to keep with you, when going through your prison your main goal is keeping your sanity!

This book was definitely a healing tool for my soul. If you have not learned anything from this read, then please learn this, no matter what the situation is, God will get you thru the storm. Do not forget who made you.

You must remember that different experiences enhance you to grow into your being. I always thought of myself as a diamond in the rough. I always thought I was a star to myself no matter what others taught. The lesson I want you to get:

Honesty

Determination

Haters

Faith

Family

Friends Forever

The Most Important One Is God

These different lessons taught me something different in every aspect. I never two faced myself or gave up on me. Sometimes people will not remain committed to what's important. In this lifetime, some people don't value true friendship. Keep in mind to always follow your gut. Life is so precious, you only get one shot at this life time. (Experiences) don't let it slide by you!! Do your best in every situation. As for me; my own personal relationship with the Mayor, shaped and made me grow as a woman of purpose. I know I made some mistakes, but my mistakes do not define me as a woman. It made me better. We must remember, going through certain situations in life, push us to become better human beings. When you know better, you do better.

My situation placed me in the path of my husband even though I did not think I would entertain the notion of ever being a wife. I did not know the place but God Did!! My Husband; John. H. McReynolds was a gift from God. He came by special delivery because I didn't see him coming at all. Mr. McReynolds is truly a man of God that stands on his belief. He is no follower of man, but a follower of God. What I learned by being with Pastor, I made sure I was a sponge for knowledge. He opened me up on an educational level about God, he didn't make it complicated but simple. He stood by me no matter what people said about me when he turned on the television. The media talked about me like a dog in the gutter. He never judged me. He always encouraged me. He cherished my being. He knew he wanted me to be his wife when I didn't. He instilled so much faith in my walk. Pastor always talked about the ram in the bush. Lord knows he knew what he was talking about.

Let's Think For A Second:

 # 1. I caught a Federal Case

 # 2. Went to court every day of the trial

#3. Was found Guilty

#4. I was sent to prison in West Virginia

#5. People called to give Press Reports as if they were reporters for channel 5.

92

After reviewing all of this, what man in his right mind hangs in there to support a convict that was a national press event? What man stands by a woman sent to Prison for over 10 months? What man would wait for her to return from Federal Prison? It does not happen. This man allowed me to know when you pray, there no need to worry. That sounds easy to do but if you don't know Jesus, or know your level of faith, you will lose. My Husband had dreams for us even when I wasn't in the position to dream for myself.

During my trial, it was a dark and lonely place because it seemed as if everyone turned their back on me. I thank God for my parents. That told me I was somebody no matter what anyone in the streets think. Pastor McReynolds, I salute you for walking the concrete jungle with me. Thank you for holding the umbrella for me when it was storming. Thank You for the protection you put around me. Thank you for never giving up on me, no matter the calls you received or what you saw on the TV. Thank you for standing as a man of God first and seeing the truth. When people told you, I was going away for a long time, you said, "no she's not." You prayed for me when I could not pray for myself. You prayed for me when I didn't know how. You never waiver in your faith, and you never stopped believing in me when you didn't even know me. Going to prison and leaving you and my family was the hardest thing to do. Taking that ride to prison was an experience of a lifetime, but you never gave up on me. This letter is to you, Pastor John H. McReyonlds.

Thank You!! Thank You! Thank You!! My Husband, My Friend and My Pastor, I love you with all of my Heart.

To the Diva Cham:

This note is to say thank you Sis! I know I have said it time after time, but I had to write it down. Sis, you were there all the way, never looked back, you never gave up on me and you made sure I was alright the whole time! Sometimes you think you know the people you call your sisters all your life and then the fairy tale sisters itself, and reality hits like a train wreck. Diva, you cannot be replaced. You are one of a kind that has always told me the truth! Love ya Cham – Always, stay true to the game! Love you sis!

To the Diva Ree:

What else can I say about the other sister I never had. Diva, you are something special to have endured a true journey with the darkest nightmare that came upon us. You are extremely someone special in my life and I am truly thankful for your being. Diva, this trial was the worst thing I have ever experienced in my whole entire life and you were right there with In-dy, Erica, Walter and Celeste. I love you from the bottom of my heart, Thanks sis! I will never forget what you did for me by going through the fire with me!

Ree and Cham:

My thank you letter to my friends Cham and Ree that rode all the way to drop me off to Prison. Let me be clear, they may not always go to the grocery store with me, or to the mall but they come out when I need them the most. That word friend has so much meaning, sometimes people do not respect the definition. I have learned even with them we had our disagreements but I never had to delete them. They are my real sisters with no biological connection... I can take them all the way to the Bank...

Please look up the word friend and it did not change in the dictionary, but many times people will use that word lightly. It's not cool to act like something you are not. I dedicate this section of my book to two Divas that I love with all my heart. Cham what can I say - you are my sister, my friend and most importantly you are a woman of character that stands tall!! I love you Diva, don't ever change, God has so many good things in store for you. Get ready publisher!

Ree, your loving spirit has carried you with the growth of your being, you are a remarkable woman. Keep staying focused, your happiness is right there. I want to thank you for your friendship and rocking it out!! Love You Diva!!

Thank you letter to my Dad:

Daddy, Daddy - You are my father and I am so thankful to have you in my life. Dad; the words, the lessons, the confidence, you had kept me alive. You never gave up on me! I know this trial was hard, not only for me, but I felt the pain it caused you! I am your daughter and no matter what the circumstances were, you never left my side. We have had our ups and downs but when I got in trouble, daddy you were there right by my side! I love you so much daddy, for never giving up on me! Thank you!

Dear Mother Mason:

This is a thank you note, I wanted printed in my book to tell you again how much I love you! I have not been in your life for a long period of time, but it seems timeless. You are one human being, God blessed me with and for that I am so thankful. I am always thanking you for pressing number five, just to hear my voice for that short period of time. Thank you for not giving up on me! Love you from the bottom of my heart!

Letter of Thanks to my Mother:

Hey mommy, it has not been all good between us, but you are still my mother and I love you. If it wasn't for you and daddy, I would not be here! This has been a hard journey for me, but God kept me! Just needed to say thanks mom, and I love you! No matter what, you are my mother and I love you dearly!

Thank You to My Dear Friends:

Monique and Felicia or Felicia and Monique:

It does not matter which name come first, because both of you were right there for me! Divas, I just needed to say thank you for being who you are, no matter what was on the table. Thank you, Fe and Mo for standing by my side. I love you Divas. Let's make it happen!

Mego and Donna:

A special note to my God brother, rest in peace Mego, and my God sister Donna! I had to write something about two people that stood strong no matter what they heard or saw on TV. Mego and Donna; just a note to say thank you for holding me down! I will never forget the conversation I had with Mego. I said to him; "Why the hell is this happening to me?" And he said; "Why not you?" I said; what is that? He kept me smiling every time I was with him. I miss you so much, rest well - Love You!

Donna, I must thank you again for making a special trip to my house and bringing some Crown Chicken on your lunch. I Know you are tired of me thanking you, but I will continue to thank you no matter what - Love You Diva!

Journal Entry: August 25, 2012

I would like to thank who ever judged me. I can honestly say, I am grateful for the haters and the supporters. The haters have no idea the strength they gave me. My supporters, I thank you for just standing in your own accord.

Now that the trial is behind me but never forgotten, the memory of each second, each minute, each hour, was well worth it. The lesson of what I went through of becoming the best woman I can be, is an everyday process. I am working at it each and every day learning to be the best I can be no matter what. I must say, I truly love my life and what comes with it. This journey has played a significant part. I have experienced some up and downs. One thing I can say, I have enjoyed the ride, even when it was bumpy and smooth.

Journal Entry: September 2012

Let me reintroduce myself, at the last chapter of this book. I am Tamika Riley McReynolds. I am a woman from Jersey City, New Jersey. I am publicist, wife, step mom, and a child of God. I do not have a whole lot of religion, but I asked God to keep working on me because I am working on me. I am a work in progress. I am a woman that have parents that love me for who I am and made me the woman I have become. I am a woman that is a force to be reckoned with. I have been all over the world, by the grace of God. I have worked with high profile people and celebrities that made me grow to make a difference in my professional journey. I have worked my butt off to be the best person I can be. I am Tamika Riley, I sometimes get scared, make mistakes, and sometimes I might have to curse you out and ask God for forgiveness. I am Tamika Riley, the woman who has taken chances in this lifetime and still not even close to being done.

One thing I can honestly say about myself is, I am a little crazy, but If I got you I got you. I am known for being a giver, stubborn and pretty much saying exactly what I feel. I am not saying it's always right, but I am telling you the truth. The other introduction, I Tamika Riley a hard-determined worker. I do not let anything get in the way of achieving the positive goals that come to be. I do not let man try to discourage or hate on me. I truly keep it moving and ask God to show me the way. If you do not know me, please don't judge me. Come see me! Let's have lunch, so you can draw your own conclusions. One thing my parents taught me was, don't be a follower, always be a leader. With this I have learned, sometimes you must follow in order to lead. I Tamika Riley am a positive force that just wants to make a difference.

I am not afraid of going after what I want to make our youth feel empowered. God has truly given me a gift, and I embrace it and thank God for it!

This Introduction of Tamika Riley is really Simple
Let me list some adjectives:

Determined

Spoiled

Empowered

Courageous

Defiant (sometimes)

Concerned

Loving

Giving

These adjectives, just to list a few, but sometimes I am not nice if I am pushed!!

Sometimes we can get out of pocket. I am that person as well, but if you know me, I got your back to the end. I truly appreciate this, God had given me and to respect it. God Thank You!!!

You have to own your being. You have to take the good with the bad. Sometimes, I know my mouth is not nice, especially when I think you want to get over!! I asked God for help, because I can let you have it without blinking. But I own it. I love the bad, the good and the indifference of Tamika Riley. If you don't, guess what? It's ok with me.

The intro to the girl, the teenager and now the woman, well It's something, when you can look back to the past, the present and look forward to the future. It's an honor, because God knows he has worked on me! I learned at an early age, we do not have to take no mess and God has the final answer. We do not have to give up on our dreams. I have remained the same chic from Jersey City. I have worked for everything I have received, trained, taught + love to remind me I can do and be whatever I want to be!!

Tamika Riley is one of a kind, you will not meet another crazy chic like myself. (Thank God) I always tell people if nobody loves you Diva, you have to love yourself in spite of it all. Please remember, God made us with different gifts and put us here to fulfill our purpose. We all must find our purpose in life and then put it to use. You cannot be jealous of the next person. Keep it moving and find your way!

I keep trying to understand why this project took so long to finish. I am reminded of the answer, when I think back a few years reading the Star Ledger back on July 30, 2008, regarding the Honorable and I. For whatever reason, everything has been moving steady in my life except this part of my life. I finally realized it is not about me. "Get over yourself Tamika," I said to myself, as I sat at my white marble dining room table.

So many times, we tried to get it together and make this book happen, well guest what... It's Here!!! The birds were singing, I was dancing, and my husband was preaching. I finally let go of anger, bitterness, hurt and opened up to forgiveness for me, so I can create my best life's work. I finally realized, I have a lot of work to do and just like you. I will finish this book no matter what. It won't be perfect but at least I know it will be completed.

Understand, tears will trickle, flood, and overwhelm at times, if they don't, you are going to explode. The unlimited emotions are so high, it makes you terrified. The emotions drive you to reach unmeasured levels of consciousness. Think positive and see your victory. It will come.

It hit me like a tornado, this case really did something to me. I dealt humbly the hand I was given but I never had the opportunity to deal with the aftermath. I know how to shut down and I have mastered that technique. I am not saying it works for everybody, but it worked for me at the time. Dealing with this major fight, I had to take on battles that were not fair and it made me lose apart of myself. The tears wouldn't stop, even though I was moving forward in a positive manner. I am still angry, I still have thoughts of hurt and I still cry. I held this inside for so long it feels like yesterday. I can now connect the act with the lesson and I have come to a level of peace with everything that has happened to me. I have accepted it and I continue to own it. I am learning to keep it in its place.

Those thoughts must be compartmentalized in your mind for you to move on. I am learning, I will never forget it because it truly helps me deal with my life on an everyday basis. It helps me to grow and to learn how to put it behind me! Lord knows it is hard each and every day. I thank God for giving me strength and the wisdom to get through the day. I thank God for getting me thru this day. The worst is over and now I am able to begin living again and making things happen the best way I know how, for my community and children. I want to continue my purpose in changing the world just a little for our youth. This experience has helped me to not give up on me. It has helped me not to give up on life and to help others.

God did not make a mistake when he made us. He knew exactly what he was doing, and my God wants us to live our best life. My daddy always says, "your body is longer dead than alive. Once it's over, it over!! Keep it moving!! In order to keep it moving, I must always remember to do what works for me and only for me. When you are faced with trials, you must still hold on. One thing I learned you must always do, is stand for you. When you think others got your back, don't be surprised if they don't. You will realize this lesson throughout your life. The only one you can depend on, is yourself.

Every day I still walk in my high heels and I realized that no one walked in my shoes but me. My experience was only for me not you. They said things and did not even know Tamika Riley. This is why I completed this book and unleashed my story because to all the HATERS, it is really simple, you can tell your story walking... Go tell THAT!!!

Thank You For Everyone That Said A Simple Prayer For Me!!!!

These are the words I used to help me break through

-Tamika Riley-McReynolds-

To be prepared for the Journey ahead. Here are the terms that helped me to withstand and go through. Define them for yourself. You will require them on your way to purpose.

It is up to you to inspire yourself to complete your mission

Determined:

Empowered:

Courageous:

Concerned:

Loving:

Giving:

Faith:

Family:

Honesty:

Determination:

Haters:

Truth:

Character:

Favor:

Loyalty:

Integrity:

Friendship:

Forgiveness:

The Five keys to a fulfilled life

1. Follow your Destiny and those things you are passionate about

2. Your Strength comes from within

3. Move forward but always put God first

4. What you think about yourself will determine your outcome

5. Despite it all you can live in your truth

My Personal List of Lessons:

- Fight for your freedom
- Determination is within
- Stand in the mist of adversity
- Validation is free
- Complete what you started
- Finish with integrity
- Motivate others from your journey

This Your Personal Journal

It is up to you to tell your story. There is no better time than NOW!

Journal Entry: Date:

Journal Entry: **Date:**

_____

_____

_____

_____

_____

_____

_____

_____

_____

_____

_____

_____

_____

_____

_____

_____

_____

_____

_____

_____

_____

_____

Journal Entry:

Date:

_____

_____

_____

_____

_____

_____

_____

_____

_____

_____

_____

_____

_____

_____

_____

_____

_____

_____

_____

_____

_____

_____

_____

Journal Entry: **Date:**

_____

_____

_____

_____

_____

_____

_____

_____

_____

_____

_____

_____

_____

_____

_____

_____

_____

_____

_____

_____

_____

_____

_____

Journal Entry: **Date:**

_____

_____

_____

_____

_____

_____

_____

_____

_____

_____

_____

_____

_____

_____

_____

_____

_____

_____

_____

_____

_____

Journal Entry: **Date:**

_____

_____

_____

_____

_____

_____

_____

_____

_____

_____

_____

_____

_____

_____

_____

_____

_____

_____

_____

_____

Journal Entry: **Date:**

_____

_____

_____

_____

_____

_____

_____

_____

_____

_____

_____

_____

_____

_____

_____

_____

_____

_____

_____

_____

Journal Entry: **Date:**

_____

_____

_____

_____

_____

_____

_____

_____

_____

_____

_____

_____

_____

_____

_____

_____

_____

_____

_____

_____

_____

_____

Journal Entry: **Date:**

_____

_____

_____

_____

_____

_____

_____

_____

_____

_____

_____

_____

_____

_____

_____

_____

_____

_____

_____

_____

Journal Entry: **Date:**

_____

_____

_____

_____

_____

_____

_____

_____

_____

_____

_____

_____

_____

_____

_____

_____

_____

_____

_____

_____

_____

Journal Entry: Date:

_____

_____

_____

_____

_____

_____

_____

_____

_____

_____

_____

_____

_____

_____

_____

_____

_____

_____

_____

_____

_____

Journal Entry: **Date:**

_____

_____

_____

_____

_____

_____

_____

_____

_____

_____

_____

_____

_____

_____

_____

_____

_____

_____

_____

_____

_____

_____

_____

Journal Entry: **Date:**

_____

_____

_____

_____

_____

_____

_____

_____

_____

_____

_____

_____

_____

_____

_____

_____

_____

_____

_____

_____

_____

Journal Entry: **Date:**

_____

_____

_____

_____

_____

_____

_____

_____

_____

_____

_____

_____

_____

_____

_____

_____

_____

_____

_____

_____

Journal Entry: **Date:**

_____

_____

_____

_____

_____

_____

_____

_____

_____

_____

_____

_____

_____

_____

_____

_____

_____

_____

_____

_____

Journal Entry: **Date:**

_____

_____

_____

_____

_____

_____

_____

_____

_____

_____

_____

_____

_____

_____

_____

_____

_____

_____

_____

_____

_____

_____

About the Author

Tamika Riley-McReynolds has worn many titles in her life. She is a successful business woman, a captivating speaker, public relations specialist, and a community leader/activist. Currently, she is the Youth Opportunity Coordinator & The Aide To The Mayor for the City Of Jersey City under the direction of Mayor Steven M. Fulop. However, the title she carries with the utmost pride and distinction is, First Lady of the Mount Olive Baptist Church in Jersey City NJ, where her husband, John H. McReynolds is the Senior Pastor.

As CEO of TRI, Inc., a boutique public relations firm, Tamika represented clients such as Ne-Yo, JaRule, Jaheim, former NBA player Eric Williams, the late Jersey City Mayor Glenn D. Cunningham, and McDonald's Franchisee Michale McGuire, just to name a few. She has worked on community projects involving Jadakiss, Queen Latifah, Sean "Diddy" Combs, Russell Simmons, Yandy Smith, NJ State Senator Sandra Cunningham, and NJ Congressman Donald Payne.

In July 2007, Tamika Riley "caught a case"; she was indicted with charges related to her romantic involvement with the legendary former Mayor of Newark, New Jersey. As a result of this federal witch hunt and prosecution, she did over 9 months Federal Prison. During that time, Tamika proved to be a conqueror! While graciously serving her time, she resolved within herself that her talents and resources would be dedicated to aiding and supporting incarcerated women transition back into society. It was imperative to Tamika that these women were able to regain and/or obtain success as it relates to self-esteem, parenting, marital support, job training, and job placement.

Upon her release, Tamika returned to her hometown of Jersey City, where she married the esteemed pastor of Mt .Olive Baptist Church, Rev John H. McReynolds. Through her mission and commitment as First Lady, she has taken great pride in mentoring the youth and creating a year-round literacy program servicing the children of Jersey City. Because of the program's continued success, the Jersey City Superintendent of schools, Dr. Marcia Lyles, has adopted and Rock for our youth here in our City!!!!!!

In addition, Mrs. McReynolds serves as a Board Member of Care Point Health Care, as well as Senator Cunningham's Woman's Advisory Group; she spearheads several other annual initiatives throughout the city, including toy drives for less fortunate children and "Back to School" supplies giveaways. She has partnered with organizations like the Hudson County Prosecutor's Office, The York Street Project and Toys for Tots, as well as McDonald's and Target. One of her most accomplished initiatives is the holiday stuffed animal giveaway at the Jersey City Medical Center, in their Pediatric ICU unit. Most recently, Tamika Riley Mc-Reynolds has been invited by former Governor James McGreevy, as a speaker on several panel discussions; supporting his nationally recognized Prisoner Re-Entry Program that was noted by former US Attorney General, Eric Holder, as a "National model" for re-entry platforms. Currently, Tamika is working with the producers of the McDonald's Gospel Fest and Bishop Hezekiah Walker on numerous community enterprises that will service Communities!!!!Their overall mission is to host conversations within the community to address relevant issues such as gun violence, and exposing our youth to positive opportunities.

Because of her tireless work, dedication, and commitment to community service, First Lady McReynolds has been recognized during Women's History Month with a Community Award presented by County Executive Tom DeGise, as well as being honored by Jersey City Mayor Steven M. Fulop with the 2018 Woman of Action Award. Collectively, Mr. and Mrs. McReynolds have received dozens of citations and proclamations from their local, state, and federal elected officials recognizing their work in the community. All of this, it is real simple, she ROCKS for our youth!!!!!!

Special Thanks To:

My Husband, Pastor John H. Reynolds

My Dad, My Mom

Gerald Krovatin, Attorney At Law

Chris Davitt & The Dream Team

Bishop Hezekiah Walker

Yandy Smith, "Love & Hip Hop"

Dr. Cissy Houston

Michale McGuire

Senator Sandra Cunningham

Jim McGreevy, Former Gov.

Felicia Smith

Ree Lawrence

Mother Deborah Mason

Francine Dawkins

Daniel Ivy

Donna O'Neill

Rasheen Peppers

Monique Smith, Hair and Makeup Stylist

Amy Ernest, MAC Celebrity Makeup Artist

Don Sherrill, Celebrity Photographer

Tishonda Carson

Wednesday Johnson

Katrinda Allen Lee

Tamika Riley - McReynolds

Sakeema James

Rudy Snelling, Jr.

Matthew Kirkwood

Credits – Special Thanks

Francine Dawkins, Shadegreen Publishing

(shadegreenpublishing@gmail.com)

Pamela Reid, Name Of The Book – "From Federal Prison To First Lady"

Don Sherrill, Celebrity Photographer, Photo For Back Cover & Bio

Felicia Smith, Long Time Hairstylist,

Hair & Makeup for back cover photo

Monique Smith, Stylist and Hair Stylist

Book Editing and Formatting AJ Houston (ajwordartist@gmail.com)

Cover Design Grace Cano @ Lushbrand.com

A special thank you to my sister, my diva, my soldier and my very true friend Cham but your real name is Francine Dawkins. Let me be extremely clear, you rocked for me during this journey and this book From Federal Prison To First Lady. It would not have happened without you. You held me down and never gave up on me. Your mother, our mother is looking down at you and just smiling at her baby girl for the accomplishments. I love you sis, YOU ROCK!!

Contact Information:

Tamika Riley - McReynolds

http://www.instagram.com/tamikamcreynolds

Email: Lady_Mcreynolds@yahoo.com

Thank you for your support

Made in the USA
Monee, IL
24 May 2021